Talking about
Trauma & Change

A Connecting Paradigms' Supplement

Matthew S. Bennett

Copyright © 2018 by Matthew S Bennett

All rights reserved.

First Printing, 2018

Bennett Innovation Group, L3C
Denver, Colorado

www.connectingparadigms.org

Books may be purchased in quantity and/or special sales by contacting the publisher by email at matt@bigl3c.org.

I dedicate this book to you. If you are reading these words, you care enough about someone else to take time to help them heal and change. For that, I thank you dearly

Table of Content

INTRODUCTION 6

PART 1: SETTING THE STAGE 12

Chapter 1: Connecting Paradigms Overview 13

Chapter 2: How to Use A Connecting Paradigms' Supplement: Talking about Trauma & Change 21

PART 2: TALKING ABOUT TRAUMA 26

Chapter 3: Introducing Trauma and Neurobiology 28

Chapter 4: Homeostasis and Epigenetics 42

Chapter 5: The Biological Injury Analogy 47

Chapter 6: The Cup Analogy 51

PART 3: TALKING ABOUT CHANGE 59

Chapter 7: Elephant and Rider 60

Chapter 8: Teaching the Stages of Change 66

Chapter 9: Social Networks and Change 85

PART 4: THE HERO'S JOURNEY 91

Chapter 10: Introduction to the Hero's Journey 95

Chapter 11: Descent into Darkness 98

Chapter 12: Suffering, Challenges, and the Soul 104

Chapter 13: Challenges, Addiction, and Trauma 108

Chapter 14: The Hero, the Mentor, and the Abyss 123

Chapter 15: Establishing Hope 128

Chapter 16: Alchemy of Transformation 133

Chapter 17: Transformation: The Alchemy of Mindfulness Part I–Mindful Practice 137

Chapter 18: Transformation: The Alchemy of Mindfulness Part II–Mindful Coping Skills 143

Chapter 19: Transformation: Mindsight 150

Chapter 20: Transformation: Empowering the Mind to Change the Brain 152

Chapter 21: Post-traumatic Growth 154

Chapter 22: The Return 157

CONCLUSIONS 159

ABOUT THE AUTHOR 161

BIBLIOGRAPHY 162

Introduction

As I wrote the first draft of Connecting Paradigms: A Trauma-Informed & Neurobiological Framework for Motivational Interviewing Implementation (Bennett, 2017), I quickly realized that I had way too much material for just one book. In my trainings, I rely heavily on analogies and models to bring the complexity and intensity of trauma and neurobiology to life. Working to integrate these into the book, I soon realized that they were distracting from the main points I was attempting to communicate concisely. Sacrificing allegory for preciseness, I cut out this material.

The result was a much better book. However, I had a nagging feeling that there was still a role for all the material that fell to the cutting-room floor. After publishing Connecting Paradigms: A Trauma-Informed & Neurobiological Framework for Motivational Interviewing Implementation, I returned to this content, trying to figure out if it could come together in a meaningful way.

Around this time, I was also being asked to do more trauma trainings for clients receiving services. I struggled initially about how to approach these trainings. Should I facilitate as I would group therapy? Or should I approach these opportunities in a similar way to how I train professionals? A friend and therapist who asked me to do a series of training for clients in a residential substance-abuse program answered this for me when she merely stated, "Just be Matt; they need the same material and energy you give professionals."

I prepared as I would for any other training: customized my slides, rehearsed, and presented my material on trauma as I would for professionals. I realized about halfway through my presentation that something powerful was happening. The energy in the room changed; most were either on the edge of their seat or sitting back in contemplation. As a trainer, you learn to realize when an audience is with you; however, it was not until afterward that I realized the full impact of this experience on all of us.

The conversations I had after the trainings taught me a couple of valuable lessons. First, there is incredible power in helping someone understand how their traumatic past is affecting them in the present. After these trainings, I hear feedback such as "I realize for the first time in my life that I'm not a bad person" or "Now I understand why my case manager thinks therapy could benefit my family" over and over again. Something about this material was liberating and motivated many to engage in mental-health services in order to heal from their past suffering and get their children help as well.

The second lesson was that many of the analogies and models that did not make it into the book resonated powerfully with client audiences. I realized that professionals could use this material to teach clients about the effects of their traumatic past and help them better understand how to make successful life changes. It became clear that I needed to get this material out.

Talking about Trauma & Change: A Connecting Paradigms' Supplement is designed to complement the material in Connecting Paradigms: A Trauma-Informed & Neurobiological Framework for Motivational Interviewing Implementation. The book provides the science, research, and practical tools that helpers need to understand their clients and implement best practices to promote healing and change. I hope that someone can pick this supplement up and find it useful as a stand-alone book. However, my primary goal is to give those who have read Connecting Paradigms: A Trauma-Informed & Neurobiological Framework for Motivational Interviewing Implementation tools for communicating its content to their clients and others in their community who might benefit from this understanding of trauma and neurobiology.

This supplement has four parts. Part 1: Setting the Stage provides a brief overview of Connecting Paradigms: A Trauma-Informed & Neurobiological Framework for Motivational Interviewing Implementation. If you have just completed the book, you can probably skip the first chapter. If you finished it a while ago, this chapter will serve as a quick refresher for the terminology and language used in the book, as well as in this supplement. After this review, I will present my thoughts on the best way to implement this material. I hope that, with a little guidance, you can integrate the content in congruence with the communication approaches presented in the book.

Part 2: Talking about Trauma explores different analogies and models to help clients learn and reflect on their lives and traumatic pasts. In the early drafts of Connecting Paradigms:

A Trauma-Informed & Neurobiological Framework for Motivational Interviewing Implementation, the analogies and models presented in this section played a significant role in how I organized the book. While it made sense to cut them out, I was thrilled that I now had a chance to share them here in a more practical context.

The third section, Part 3: Talking about Change, provides several analogies and models that complement the context presented in the book. Since we explored Motivational Interviewing (MI) in detail in the book, the information presented in this supplement is designed to complement MI while not duplicating any material. The focus of Part 3 is on how to help clients understand the change process and the neurobiological adjustments needed to support behavioral change.

The final section, Part 4: The Hero's Journey, presents a model that I use frequently in my trainings with both staff and clients in services. The hero's journey brings together critical aspects of the healing and change process so clients can identify where they are in their journeys to healing and growth and what they need to focus on to successfully take their next step. This model provides many great opportunities for us to help clients gain insight and self-understanding while eliciting change talk about living the life they desire.

Language of Talking about Trauma and Change

Throughout Talking about Trauma & Change: A Connecting Paradigms' Supplement, I will reference material presented in Connecting Paradigms: A Trauma-Informed & Neurobiological

Framework for Motivational Interviewing Implementation. To avoid confusion and help the flow of my writing, I will use the word "book" when referring to Connecting Paradigms: A Trauma-Informed & Neurobiological Framework for Motivational Interviewing Implementation. I will use the word "supplement" when talking about this work.

The information presented throughout this supplement can be applied in different settings and by a diverse range of professionals who work with people trying to make positive life changes and overcome past suffering and trauma. Each environment has its unique language and terminology. This book uses language that strives to be universal and applicable in all these unique situations.

This supplement will use the word "client" to describe a person in services or programs. The word "client" may also represent patients in a healthcare setting, students in school settings, or participants in social-service programs. The term "helper" is used to describe those who interact with clients.

You will notice one significant difference between the language in this supplement and the book. Here, I write in a voice as if I am communicating directly with clients. I hope that you use this supplement like a workbook where you can hand out sections or entire chapters as a group activity or homework. While this book is copyrighted, I give you permission to duplicate, customize, and be innovative with all the material in these pages. Please reference it appropriately and use it liberally!

While the supplement is written in a conversational style to support implementation, each chapter includes a section called Matt's Notes. In these sections, I am talking directly to you. In Matt's Notes, I share my personal experiences with the content and provide you with ideas for effective implementation. I hope that sharing my thoughts and experiences assists you in getting the most out of the material.

A Final Word about You

If I am effective in presenting this material, it should not only speak to our client's experience, but to ourselves and those we love. While I focus time in every section and chapter on hope and opportunities for growth, reading about trauma is always difficult. If any of the content feels like it is too close to home and makes you depressed or anxious, take a break, a deep breath or two, or a walk around the block, or share the experience with a friend or loved one. For some, this material might bring up issues such as traumatic memories. If that is the case, please seek out a mental-health professional. As we showed in the book, if a person gets the right support and resources, trauma is transformed from pain and suffering into wisdom and strength.

Part 1: Setting the Stage

The book brought together different paradigms and research areas to create an innovative approach to helping clients with traumatic histories heal from their past trauma and make difficult life changes. This exploration spanned many complex topics, including neurobiology, epigenetics, intergenerational genetic expression, attachment, and neuroplasticity. This knowledge set the foundation and justification for the practical approaches, including MI, stages of change, harm reduction, mindfulness, and mindsight.

Part 1: Setting the Stage has two chapters. In the first chapter, we review the research and paradigms by doing a quick summary of the concepts presented in the book. The second chapter in this section will outline ideas and approaches for how to best implement the concepts presented throughout this supplement. We want to be strategic in how we structure discussions concerning change and trauma, as there is always the potential to retraumatize people, elicit resistance, or contribute to disengagement. The key to our success is not just what we say, but how we say it.

Chapter 1: Connecting Paradigms Overview

In the first chapter, I will provide a brief overview of the concepts covered in the book. In case it has been a while since you have read the book, what follows is a quick review to ensure we are working off of a shared language and understanding. If you have just completed the book, you can skip the following few pages and go directly to Chapter 2.

The Trauma-Informed Paradigm

Two-thirds of the people in your community have experienced something that potentially results in decreased life expectancy, cancer, HIV, poverty, incarceration, domestic violence, and homelessness. The experience at the root of all these social and public health issues is trauma. For some, trauma is an event that causes temporary pain and suffering and, if provided with the right support, eventually results in increased levels of resiliency (Centers for Disease Control and Prevention, 2016).

Unfortunately, most people experiencing homelessness, extreme poverty, mental-health struggles, incarceration, and addiction never had an opportunity to heal and recover, resulting in a life dominated by the pain and suffering of trauma. Just as we should not blame the person for having trauma inflicted on them, we should not blame them for the behaviors, mental-health issues, medical issues, and social struggles resulting from traumatic experience, if they do not get the help they need to recover. Our challenge is to help those people in a way that stops the pain and gives them an opportunity to live the lives they deserve.

Trauma and Human Development

Human beings are social creatures. We thrive in healthy relationships. Unfortunately, most trauma occurs when one person with power violates the dignity of another person, inflicting tremendous pain and suffering. When relationships, especially in childhood, that should be nurturing and supportive become dangerous and traumatic, it disrupts healthy brain development. Through the processes of epigenetics, neurogenesis, and pruning, the brain adapts to traumatic environments in a way that supports survival and reactivity (Bloom, 2000; Bloom & Farragher, 2011)

Overdevelopment of survival areas of the brain comes at a cost, as the areas associated with emotional regulation and cognitive ability weaken. An unfortunate effect of being in traumatic relationships and situations is that people establish a relationship template based on believing that all people are potential sources of harm. The good news is that if someone with compassion and patience can build a healthy relationship with the individual, the brain can heal and relationship templates change as the client sees that not all people are bad and out to hurt them (Nakazawa, 2016; Ogden, Minton, & Pain, 2006).

The Brain and Trauma

Unhealed trauma becomes a biological injury. The brain adapts to survive traumatic situations and high-stress environments. While this adaptation promotes survival, the person will struggle with activities necessary for success in academics and employment. Without the right type of assistance, the neurobiological impact of trauma often results in behaviors and ways of thinking and feeling that keep people stuck in unhealthy situations. A basic understanding of the brain demonstrates the devastation of trauma and why it can negatively affect a client's ability to realize the life they want to live (Nakazawa, 2016; Ogden, Minton, & Pain, 2006).

Basics of Motivational Interviewing

William R. Miller and Stephen Rollnick (2012), the founders of Motivational Interviewing or MI, provide this definition of their approach:

> Motivational Interviewing is a collaborative, goal-oriented style of communication with particular attention to the language of change. It is designed to strengthen personal motivation for and commitment to a specific goal by eliciting and exploring the person's reasons for change within an atmosphere of acceptance and compassion.

The Spirit of MI ensures that communication focuses on creating partnerships, evoking the expertise that lies within the client, accepting that the client is where they are in life and working from that point, and approaching our work with compassion. The strategies of the Spirit of MI provide an ideal intervention for those struggling with past trauma. MI is a best practice that helps reach through the pain and suffering of trauma and supports the client in a way that promotes change and healing (Miller & Rollnick, 2012; Murphy, 2008).

The Mind and Stages of Change

"Losing one's mind" is a real consequence of trauma. The neurobiological damage of trauma makes it difficult for people to control their emotions and behaviors. People struggling with homelessness, extreme poverty, violence, addiction, and other intense issues face making many changes to improve their situations. Those helping them need a strategic way to assess where to begin conversations around change. Understanding how the mind can gain control of emotions and behaviors is a critical step in the journey to change and healing. The concept of stages of change provides a structure to visualize the change process and implement interventions that help clients effectively navigate their change. At the same time, the stages of change help clients avoid the common pitfalls that can lead to disengagement and resistance (Prochaska, DiClemente, & Norcross, 1992; Schwartz & Begley 2002; Siegel, 2016).

MI Process: Engage

The greater the client's engagement in their change and the services designed to help them accomplish their change, the more likely they are to achieve positive results. Unfortunately, many traditional approaches diminish engagement, lead to resistance, or, even worse, result in people dropping out of services altogether. MI uses four communication approaches—open-ended questions/statements, affirmations, reflections, and summaries–to build and maintain engagement and to strengthen the helping relationships. These approaches are simple to learn and implement and are utilized heavily in all the strategies presented in the book (Miller & Rollnick, 2012).

Trust and Safety

MI and trauma-informed practices rely heavily on the trust and safety established between the client and us. Due to the pain and suffering inflicted on the client during traumatic experiences, building trust and psychological safety are difficult. To make matters worse, many people are in unsafe physical situations due to experiencing homelessness, domestic violence, food scarcity, and community violence. Without trust and safety, the brain will focus on ways to best promote short-term survival, which comes at the expense of focusing on changes that would improve their condition in the long term. Building trust and safety necessitates integrating trauma-informed approaches that promote both physical and psychological safety. (Bloom, 2006; Bloom & Farragher, 2013; Stanley & Brown, 2012).

MI Process: Focus

Past suffering, lack of safety, unhealthy relationships, and the inability to see a better future all diminish a client's ability to focus on their change. MI and harm reduction are two approaches that, when combined, help both us and the client focus attention on things that will eventually result in long-term change. Meeting the client where they are in life, realizing that a client is not the embodiment of the sum of their problems, increasing safety by reducing harm, and being nonjudgmental are strategies of harm reduction, MI, and trauma-informed approaches. These all promote the client's ability to focus on more than just their survival (Marlatt, Larimer, & Witkiewitz, 2012; Miller & Rollnick, 2012; Roe, 2005).

Mindfulness

The practice of mindfulness is changing traditional views of the healing process and leading to breakthroughs in psychology and other related fields. In the book, mindfulness is presented as an activity and set of skills that help heal the traumatized brain and support the change process. While the research behind the benefits of mindfulness is substantial, many in the helping professions have struggled to introduce and practice mindfulness with the people they are serving. As a complementary tool to MI, mindfulness strengthens neurobiological processes that promote healing and change (Langer, 2009; Parnell, 2008).

MI Process: Evoke

The motivation for change comes from within the client. Each client is an expert on themselves and their situation. The success of any change emerges out of this expertise. The more a client talks about a change, the more likely that the change will happen. MI provides a set of approaches that elicit talk about a change in a way that helps people progress through the stages of change. These approaches allow people to explore their desire, reason, and need to change, while at the same time building the confidence that they can make their change a reality. Motivation builds through this exploration, eventually leading to action (Miller & Rollnick, 2012).

Mindsight

Mindsight is a deep level of insight into a client's situation that brings forth motivation for action. Mindsight helps clients see their ambivalence, their wanting more than one thing when those things are incompatible, concerning their change. While ambivalence can feel uncomfortable, this feeling creates a type of stress called cognitive dissonance, which occurs when a client realizes that they are living a life not aligned with their values or morals. Cognitive dissonance creates motivation for meaningful change, as the client attempts to remove the dissonance from their lives. The last aspect of mindsight is to move from cognitive dissonance to motivation and then to action. Put together, the steps of mindsight are potent tools for transformation and change (Dweck, 2006; Siegel, 2011).

MI Process: Plan

A plan is a set of actions and tasks that help a client move out of their current state into a better future. Few people in stressful situations possess the ability to plan in isolation. Assisting clients in creating goals and objectives to improve their safety, reduce stress, and change their condition is central to the process of healing and change. While planning can seem simple on the surface, implementing it in accordance with MI, harm reduction, and trauma-informed approaches requires skill and thought (Miller & Rollnick, 2012; Stanley & Brown, 2012).

Post-traumatic Growth

Overcoming the pain and suffering of trauma is an opportunity to gain resiliency, strength, and wisdom. This transformation is called post-traumatic growth. Everyone's journey to post-traumatic growth is unique, which challenges those helping them to find the right mix of support, strategies, and resources. One change leads to another and another; confidence builds, futures become filled with hope, and lives are transformed. The journey to post-traumatic growth for many is lengthy and requires overcoming difficult barriers, but the result for the client is nothing short of life-changing (Siebert, 2005).

Chapter 2: How to Use A Connecting Paradigms' Supplement: Talking about Trauma & Change

Addressing trauma and facing difficult life changes is overwhelming for many people. The book demonstrated how unresolved trauma hinders a client's ability to consider and successfully work through the stages of change. Helping people heal and change is a complicated process and requires a unique set of strategies, communication styles, and approaches.

This supplement is designed to provide you with a range of analogies and models that complement the strategies presented in the first book. Think of the trauma-informed paradigm and neurobiology as a tool belt. The paradigm and science give us an understanding of those we are trying to help and the tools to determine which mix of strategies and resources we need to utilize with a particular client.

The strategies and approaches presented in the book, including MI, mindfulness, stages of change, mindsight, growth mindset, and harm reduction, represent tools in your trauma-informed tool belt. These tools help you know how to communicate, create a shared agenda, and successfully partner with your client on their journey toward a better future.

Drills and screwdrivers have many different heads that you can change depending on the specifics of the task. Think of the supplement's analogies and models as interchangeable heads for these tools, complementing the main concepts in the book. The implementation of these analogies and models will help clients gain insight and understanding of themselves and the next steps of their journey to healing and change.

Formats for Implementation

As tools, the analogies and models are flexible and designed for implementation in individual conversation, group counseling or therapy, and larger psycho-educational groups or classroom settings. There are some general considerations about the format in which you implement these analogies and models.

Individual

Much of the book focused on individual work with clients in counseling, psycho-social support, medical, case-management, and therapeutic relationships. The communication skills associated with MI and Spirit of MI (partnership, compassion, evocation, and acceptance) remain the critical foundation when presenting these analogies and models. Just as with the concepts presented in the book, your success and the outcomes for the client depend heavily on the quality of the relationship.

Groups

Most of the analogies and models presented in this supplement are perfect for support and therapeutic groups for several reasons. First, they provide meaningful subject matter to structure groups. Second, they provide group members with a shared language that will increase their ability to apply the subject matter to their situation and deepen their connections with other group members. Third, they are safe ways to reflect on difficult topics in group settings. In this reflection, clients gain insight into their thinking and behavior while supporting their fellow group members in their healing and change journeys.

I developed the analogies and models for flexible implementation. Integrate them in a way that makes sense for the focus of your group and the group's dynamics. Most analogies and models work great as topics for a single group session. Some are more in-depth and are perfect for structuring months of group interactions.

As with individual work, the approaches and strategies presented in the book serve as a foundation to structure communication and to focus on building group safety and trust. Sharing traumatic histories and resulting struggles are often powerful moments in a client's healing journey. Make sure you have the right mental-health support and safety within the group before asking members to focus on or even share their traumatic experiences.

Psycho-educational Groups

Learning about trauma and why change is difficult is liberating and an essential part of many clients' healing and change journeys. For many, the intensity of individual and group therapy and processing their traumatic pasts keeps them from engaging in mental-health services. Psycho-educational groups are excellent tools to introduce personally sensitive concepts in a safe environment that helps clients gain insight into their behaviors and emotions.

Sitting in a larger group without the expectation of sharing or processing their personal experience creates a level of safety. The analogies and models presented in this supplement are ideal for this setting, as they use imagery and stories to help educate people on the complex science behind trauma and change. When conducting psycho-educational groups, it is important to have mental-health support available. These groups often help people see why it is crucial to address past trauma and they build motivation to do further work.

Setting the Stage

These analogies and models provide a safe way to consider trauma and making a difficult life change. However, when trauma is the topic, there is a high risk for retraumatization and other stress reactions that might lead to disengagement. As mentioned throughout the book, the success of any intervention is dependent more on the quality of the relationship than the technique utilized. Returning to the chapters on engagement (Chapter 6) and on trust and safety (Chapter 7) in the book will help ensure you maximize this key driver of outcomes.

This supplement presents analogies and models that any professional, regardless of training or educational level, can utilize in their work. If you are not a trained therapist or mental-health professional, it is essential to work in collaboration with one to get coaching and supervision before and during the use of these approaches. This support is critical for two reasons. First, it helps those without mental-health training to identify any possible hazards for retraumatization before implementation. Second, the goal of many of these approaches is to help the client gain insight into why engaging in mental-health services to address their trauma is crucial for not only their psychological health, but also for their success in realizing positive change in their lives. When clients have this realization, you want to make sure you can make quick and effective referrals to mental-health services.

Part 2: Talking about Trauma

The goal of Part 2: Talking about Trauma is to help you effectively share research on trauma and post-traumatic growth in a way that motivates people to take their own healing journey. As I stated in the book, understanding trauma from a neurobiological perspective is a complex and in-depth subject that took me years to fully grasp. In this part, we will use analogies and models to present the science of trauma in language that those without any background or knowledge in psychology or neurobiology can apply to their situation.

The approach is not to "dumb down" the information; this underestimates the intelligence of the audience. People grasp neurobiology quickly because they are living the experience. These analogies and models create opportunities for reflection and insight.

Trauma and our expanding knowledge of the brain will play an increasingly significant role in psychology, public health, social services, social work, education, early childhood programs, and other related professions in the future. This knowledge promotes compassion for ourselves and others. The resulting insight often transforms into motivation to change behavior, to engage in mental-health services, and to make other positive life changes.

While my message differs slightly depending on my audience, this part of the supplement presents my general approach to helping people understand the effects of trauma on their functioning and on those they love. As a reminder, from here on in the supplement, I use the voice I would implement when communicating to clients, except in the sections labeled Matt's Notes and the introductions to each part.

Chapter 3: Introducing Trauma and Neurobiology

We live in a unique time in human history. It is easy to make the argument that since 1990, we have learned more about the brain, and hence the human condition, than during all of human history up to that point. Our knowledge of brain science, or neurobiology, is transforming how we view ourselves and those we love. Exploring this science helps us understand how our past experiences might be influencing us in the present.

In this introduction to trauma and neurobiology, we will explore the effects of stress and trauma on our brains and overall health and well-being. For some, trauma is a difficult topic, as it reminds us of our past pain and suffering. Here, we will learn about trauma in a very general way, and you will not be required to share any of your previous experiences. If any of this makes you feel uncomfortable, please tell someone, as this feeling is our body's way of notifying us that we could use some support.

Trauma

Trauma is an intense type of stress that knocks us down and keeps us down for a period of time. Some people recover from trauma in a few days or weeks if the threat passes and they get the right help and support. Other people might struggle with the pain and suffering of trauma their entire lives. The goal of our exploration of trauma is to identify if we need help, connect to the right type of support, and heal, so our past does not adversely affect our future happiness and well-being.

Several different terms help distinguish between types of trauma. The first type we will call big T trauma. Big T trauma describes a traumatic event. Something terrible happens that overwhelms our ability to cope. A big T trauma dominates our thoughts and emotional well-being. It might haunt our dreams, cause us to react in ways we typically would not, and experience fear that a similar event could happen again at any time.

There is also a phenomenon termed small t trauma. Small t trauma occurs when someone lives in highly stressful or traumatic situations for extended periods of time (Lewis, 2006; Siebert, 2005). These stressful situations might include experiencing homelessness, living with the threat of abuse or domestic violence, living in an unstable and volatile family situation, struggling with addiction, living with someone abusing drugs, or surviving in extreme poverty. Big T traumas coincide with a specific time and place; small t traumas lack this specificity, but have an equally devastating effect.

Here is a quick example to show the relationship between big T trauma and small t trauma. A child is growing up in a home where her father is struggling with alcoholism. Sometimes, when he drinks too much, he becomes abusive to her and her mother. On Tuesday night, her dad goes to the bar after work and gets drunk.

When her dad returns home, he becomes furious that there is no dinner left for him. He starts yelling at the mother, who is trying her best to calm him down. The daughter hides behind her mother, wishing just to disappear. Unfortunately, the dad ends up striking the mother and spanking the daughter for no reason, and he threatens them both that it will be worse the next time his dinner is not on the table when he gets home.

This disruptive and abusive situation is a big T trauma. The daughter was scared for her and her mother's safety and could not predict the outcome of her father's rage or how bad the abuse would get. The daughter does not sleep that night, as she cannot get her father's threatening words out of her mind, and the pain of his abuse remains in her body.

Wednesday, the daughter gets up early and leaves the house before her father wakes up. Dad does not get abusive the rest of the week. However, the daughter's waking hours are filled with terror, worrying about whether her father will get drunk after work and become abusive again. She has trouble sleeping and finds it impossible to concentrate at school.

There are no traumatic events, or big T traumas, the rest of the week. However, the threat of danger and lack of safety and security create small t traumas that have biological and psychological consequences similar to those of big T trauma. When one experiences homelessness, war, or living in a violent neighborhood or home, there might not always be an event at a specific time and place that we can identify as traumatic, but the constant threat of a possible trauma becomes traumatic in and of itself.

If the father's threats and abuse continue over months or years, the totality of the daughter's experience is an example of complex trauma. Complex trauma is trauma that occurs systematically over time and involves a combination of big T and small t traumas. Complex trauma dominates the life of the survivor, as most of their focus energy is directed toward finding any safety they can in their situation (Bloom & Farragher, 2011; Herman, 1997).

Trauma is devastating on so many levels. Trauma's immediate impact is overwhelming and can lead to increased anxiety, depression, and fear. Besides the initial reactions to trauma, there are many long-term consequences of big T, small t, and complex trauma as well. The list below summarizes the research on the short- and long-term effects of trauma on the survivor.

Results of Adverse Childhood Experiences		
Inability to focus	Chronic fatigue	Anger
Learning disrupted	Feelings of detachment	Rage
Short-term memory	Depression	Fibromyalgia
Verbal memory	Suicide attempts	Unintended pregnancies
Narrative memory	Autoimmune disease	Difficulty trusting others
Limited volition	Lupus	Nightmares
Emotional instability	Asthma	Liver disease
Nightmares	Obesity	Isolation
Somatic pain	Disrupted sleep patterns	Social withdrawal
Heart attacks	Constipation or diarrhea	Illicit drug use
Fetal death	Fear	Smoking
Stroke	Anxiety	Attachment issues
Cancer	Diabetes	Flashbacks
Concern about burdening others with problems	Risk for intimate partner violence	Lack of awareness of social cues
Sexually transmitted infections (STIs)	Increased number of emergency room visits	Alcohol abuse & dependence
Decreased health-related quality of life	Disrupted personality development	Loss of positive point of view (self & world)
(*Sources:* CDC, 2016; Herman, 1997; Robert Wood Johnson Foundation, 2017; Levin, 2004; Nakazawa, 2016.)		

Neurobiology and Stress

The brain is a fascinating and complex organ. Neurobiology, or the science of the brain, provides us with critical insights into our behaviors and emotions. Let's take a moment to learn about your brain and then explain how trauma affects how the brain works.

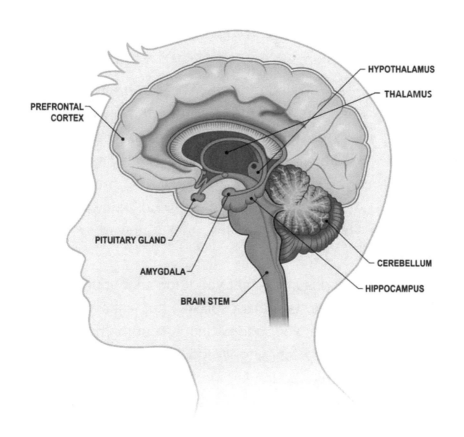

In starting our exploration, let's learn how the brain processes events that are happening in your environment. Your senses take in information and turn it into electrical pulses that travel to the different areas of your brain. The thalamus processes the senses of sound and sight (touch and smell are sent directly to the amygdala, which we'll discuss shortly) and sits in the center of the brain. One of the thalamus' main roles is to serve as the control center, deciding which parts of the brain are best suited to handle the situation you are facing. If the thalamus determines that there are no threats in the environment, the stimulus is sent to the cortex. (Courtois & Ford, 2009; Goleman, 2006; Siegel 2016; Wright, 2011).

The cortex is the wrinkled outer layer of the brain. It provides meaning to what you are experiencing in the environment by comparing your present situation to your past experiences and memories. If you have learned anything in the past about the brain, your cortex is doing this right now. It is processing the information by comparing it to existing knowledge and experiences you have had in the past (Schwartz & Begley, 2002; Siegel, 2011).

For example, I'm assuming that you know that your brain is in your head. I did not state this explicitly, but since you already have this knowledge, your cortex brings your memories on the topic to what you are learning. Without consciously reminding yourself, "Oh, my brain is in my head," your cortex automatically applies past knowledge and you know when I mention the brain that it is in your head

The cortex contains the prefrontal cortex, which is primarily responsible for making humans great thinkers and planners. The prefrontal cortex plays a significant role in reasoning, flexible problem-solving, delaying gratification, planning, and aspects of emotional regulation (Siegel, 2007). When active, the prefrontal cortex is always thinking about the best way to respond to a situation or how to apply the information you are learning.

Next, the amygdala and hippocampus are activated. These two areas help determine how you feel about a situation or what you are learning. Our feelings for things and people create an emotional experience of the world around us. Emotions are critical, as they provide us with the energy and motivation to take action toward realizing a change.

The above description was used to demonstrate the process in slow motion. In the time it took to cover this material, your brain has consistently been working on processing each word, as well as anything else going on in your environment. In this brief time, your brain has processed billions of pieces of information. If it determines that any of the information is important, the brain will turn it into a long-term memory, allowing you to recall the information when needed.

Next, let's examine what happens when the thalamus identifies that something we see or hear in the environment is a threat. When the thalamus recognizes a danger, it sends the information to the amygdala directly. The amygdala manages the emotional and behavioral responses needed for survival in the face of real or perceived threats.

Centrally positioned and highly connected to other brain areas, the amygdala is quick and decisive. In response to a threat, the amygdala signals the hypothalamus, pituitary gland, and adrenal glands to release the stress hormone cortisol. If the danger is great or traumatic, the stress hormone norepinephrine, often called adrenaline, is also released, increasing the intensity of the stress reaction even further. Cortisol and norepinephrine kick what is called the sympathetic nervous system into action (Goleman, 2006; Siegel, 2011).

Key indications of sympathetic nervous system activation are:

- Increased heart rate
- Increased blood pressure
- Shortness and quickening of breath
- Sweat and goosebumps on the skin (Ogden, Minton, & Pain, 2006)

During sympathetic nervous system activation, energy shifts from regular functions, such as digestion, sex, and thinking, into the arms and legs, so we are prepared to fight what is causing us stress or to escape from the danger. In most situations, this amygdala response will continue until the threat has passed, providing us with high levels of strength and stamina. This increase in strength and stamina is gained from powering down the cortex and prefrontal cortex. Amygdala responses are highly emotional and reactive; we might say or do things that we would not usually do when we are processing from our thinking cortex (Siegel, 2011).

The hippocampus also is a crucial player as to whether or not a threat exists. When there is no threat present, it works with the amygdala to provide an emotional context to the stimulus. The hippocampus also plays a significant role in the creation of new memories.

When there is a threat present, the hippocampus takes on a calming role. Once a threat no longer exists, the hippocampus helps to quiet the amygdala, allowing the prefrontal cortex to re-engage and cognitive functioning to return. A well-functioning hippocampus makes it possible to have a brief, intense response, which might include fear or anger, but it doesn't allow these emotions to become a permanent state of being (Cozolino, 2006; Cozolino, 2010).

Trauma and the Brain

Next, let's look at how trauma, especially complex trauma, affects brain functioning. Trauma can cause the thalamus to adjust in two ways. First, we misinterpret a nonthreatening situation as a dangerous one. When this happens, the stimulus goes to the amygdala instead of the cortex. A common saying in neurobiology goes, "It is better to run away from a stick thinking it was a snake than to pick up a snake thinking it was a stick." Many with traumatic pasts see threats and react in extreme ways, even when there is little or no chance of harm (Cozolino, 2010).

The second effect of trauma on the thalamus occurs when it misses actual threats in the environment that it should identify as dangerous. Those with traumatic histories are at a higher risk of being traumatized again, due in part to their reduced ability to sense when a situation might become harmful. Unfortunately, the inability to identify threats leads us to engage in unhealthy relationships and behaviors that end up harming us in the long run, even though, at the time, they seem harmless or even positive (Mate & Levine, 2010).

The thalamus and hippocampus play critical roles in memory development and processing. When a trauma floods the thalamus with stress hormones, it prevents the creation of fully formed memories of the traumatic event. These fragmented and incoherent memories make it difficult to make sense of the traumatic experience and leave us feeling disoriented.

The amygdala is also affected by the experience of trauma. Brain scans show that the amygdalae of individuals with traumatic histories are larger in size. A larger amygdala enhances the likelihood that the fear response will occur in everyday situations. Trauma and the effects it has on the amygdala make it difficult to perceive one's self, relationships, and the world as safe. When we feel unsafe, our amygdala is activated, leading to fear and anxiety, while taking the prefrontal cortex offline limits our ability to think logically about what is happening to us (Medina, 2014; Siegel, 2011).

While the amygdala triggers the fear response, the hippocampus attempts to regulate this response and quiet it once the danger has passed. Trauma also impairs the hippocampus, but in the opposite way that it does the amygdala. Where the amygdala becomes overactive, the hippocampus weakens and often becomes physically smaller. A weakened hippocampus makes it difficult for us to gain control over our emotions once we experience fear or anxiety. Too often, our emotions control us instead of the other way around (Ogden, Minton, & Pain, 2006).

The overactive amygdala and weaker hippocampus mean the brain does not send as much information to the cortex and prefrontal cortex. This underactivation limits our ability for logic, emotional regulation, and strategic thinking. Because the prefrontal cortex is under-engaged, it becomes weaker over time. This neurobiology reduces the activation of areas needed for us to change behaviors or think beyond our immediate situation (Ogden, Minton, & Pain, 2006; Siegel, 2011).

Retraumatization is another way that traumatic experiences affect the brain function. Retraumatization is re-experiencing the emotions and/or memories of a traumatic event. Biologically, retraumatization starts when something that is seen as neutral by the thalamus goes to the cortex. If the memory centers in the cortex connect the stimulus to past traumatic events, the cortex will immediately send energy to the amygdala, resulting in retraumatization. This trigger for retraumatization can be anything that reminds us of our past trauma, including noises, visual stimuli, or a word or tone of voice occurring in the context of a normal conversation (Siegel, 2011).

Retraumatization is designed to keep us safe from things like those that hurt us in the past. Retraumatization is sometimes called a post-traumatic stress reaction. Unfortunately, when retraumatization occurs in the context of everyday situations and relationships, it can be debilitating. Retraumatization makes it challenging to succeed in services, school, or employment when ordinary things seem potentially life-threatening to our brain.

The good news about trauma is that with the right mix of support, hard work, and resources, even the worst traumatic experience can transform into resiliency, wisdom, and growth. The term used to describe this transformation is post-traumatic growth. Like an injury to other parts of the body, traumatic injuries to the brain heal with the right treatment. Mental-health services, better living situations, new healthy relationships, drug treatment programs, medical care and medication, and other supports and resources combine to heal the wounds of trauma and create a stronger, more resilient brain.

Your treatment will be unique to your situation. It will take some hard work and effort to heal your brain and change your life. However, you are worth it, and your future happiness makes the journey one of the most powerful things any human being experiences in their life.

> Can you identify how trauma is affecting the behavior of people you know?
>
> Do you see any of the behaviors discussed in this chapter in your own reactions to stress?
>
> Have you ever felt like your emotions controlled you in a situation?

Matt's Notes

I have found providing the above information to be very useful in psycho-educational group settings. Larger groups without the requirement of therapeutic processing, where there is an expectation that clients share their traumatic experiences, allow group members to learn about "people" and not focus inwards on their trauma before they are ready. This approach permits them to apply the material to their situation in accordance with their level of comfort and readiness.

For individual and group work, especially those being done by non-therapists, I would suggest using the analogies and models in following chapters, unless you feel that you have established a high level of safety and trust and have mental-health resources available in case of retraumatization. In these more intimate settings, people are likely to feel they need to share their experiences, even if they might not feel ready.

Throughout this supplement, we will examine many ways to help communicate hope to clients by assisting them in understanding the transformational process. The takeaway challenge from this chapter is to think about how you can teach the science of trauma and neurobiology to your clients. In my work, I have found that when clients understand their brains, they start to gain tremendous insight into their behaviors and struggles.

Chapter 4: Homeostasis and Epigenetics

Your brain changes throughout your life as it adapts to changes in living situations, experiences, and relationships. While complex trauma structures the brain to stay in a reactive survival state, engaging in mental-health services, establishing a stable living environment, maintaining healthy relationships, achieving sobriety, and making other positive changes help repair the damage done by traumatic experiences. Homeostasis and epigenetics provide us with a scientific explanation behind our ever-evolving and changing brain.

Homeostasis is a big word used to describe how our brains evolve in response to our environment. If we are surviving on the streets or in a war zone, our brain will adapt to give us the best chance to survive in those traumatic settings. If we are working a full-time job and are in a loving romantic relationship, our brain will adapt to promote success in those activities. Homeostasis has allowed human beings to thrive in the freezing cold of the Arctic as well as the hottest deserts on the planet.

The ability of our brain to change and adapt throughout our lifespan is called neuroplasticity, a word used to describe the flexible or plastic nature of the brain. While our brain is always changing, these changes take time to happen. A 55-year-old nomad who lived every day of their life in the Sahara Desert would struggle to survive the Arctic if we uprooted them from their desert environment on Tuesday and dropped them in the Arctic on Wednesday.

The brain needs time to adapt. A desert nomad does not have the knowledge or skill set to survive in a new environment right away. However, with training, support, and a gradual transition, the nomad could adjust over several months (Shenk, 2010).

There is one more significant scientific finding concerning homeostasis. While the brain changes throughout one's lifespan, it develops and changes rapidly from birth to around age 25. For this reason, big T, small t, and complex traumas are especially devastating for those who experience these traumas in their childhood.

Homeostasis gives us the greatest chance of survival; it accomplishes this through the process known as epigenetics. Epigenetics is the study of how the environment interacts with our biology, expressing or suppressing specific genes in our deoxyribonucleic acid, or DNA. Most of us learned in school that the DNA we get from our parents determines our eye color, height, and the color of our skin. This type of DNA is chromosomal DNA and only accounts for less than 2% of our total DNA (Wolynn, 2016).

The other 98% of our DNA is called noncoding DNA, or ncDNA. ncDNA is highly adaptive and expresses itself differently depending on environmental factors. When the environment demands a particular skill or trait, the ncDNA releases proteins called ribonucleic acid (RNA). The RNA directs cell behavior, ultimately allowing the person to develop brain areas that support specific characteristics or traits. These traits can lead to changes in behavior that promote survival in the environment (Lipton, 2006; Wolynn, 2016). Even studies of genetically identical, cloned animals and human twins show significant differences in personality traits depending on their environments (Shenk, 2010).

If we are lucky enough to be raised in a safe and nurturing environment, we express ncDNA that helps regulate our nervous system. This regulation results in the ability to handle stress, remain cognitively engaged in a situation, and recover from stressful events more quickly (Cozolino, 2010; Siegel, 2011). In other words, loving and stable parental figures help develop wiring in the brain that allows individuals to interact well in the world of education, in employment, and in other social situations.

On the other hand, if we grow up in a dysfunctional, neglectful, and abusive environment, ncDNA releases RNA that promotes the development of the traits needed to survive these adverse situations. While the person remains in such settings, traits such as hyperalertness, being quick-tempered, or the ability to shut down emotionally will help them to survive in these harsh situations. (Sapolsky, 2017).

Even those raised in the most traumatic situations can heal their brain if they get the right support and resources. To experience post-traumatic growth, most people need safe and stable environments with people in their lives who care about them and their future. Our brain might struggle at first to adapt to the stability of this new environment, but over time it will adjust. These changes will also help the brain develop areas necessary for success in school or employment as the amygdala is less engaged and the prefrontal cortex recovers and builds strength.

Consider the following two questions:

> First, when you think about your life, can you identify any ways in which your environment and past experiences shaped your brain, personality, thinking, or behaviors?

> Second, can you identify how changes you could make in the next year might help your brain and mental health in positive ways?

Matt's Notes

Homeostasis and epigenetics provide an ideal opportunity to help the client separate their problems from whom they are as a person. Understanding that many of their struggles are natural adaptations that their brain used to survive trauma gives them permission to forgive themselves, stop their harsh self-judgment, and drop many of the societal labels that they might have internalized to their self-identity. Homeostasis and epigenetics complement the previous chapter's science on the brain by explaining how certain traits and characteristics develop.

The questions asked at the end of this section are designed to help the client reflect on their environment's influence on their mental health and life choices. I find that clients who can make this connection start to view themselves in a more positive light and begin to break out of the negative self-talk that often dominates the thinking of those with severe traumatic histories. Time spent helping clients make this connection is time well spent.

Another goal of this section is to help clients understand the importance of accessing resources. Connecting the safety and stability of the environment to their well-being often increases motivation to access services and resources that improve their living conditions. Seeing themselves as worthy human beings and being more than the sum of their problems increases motivation to take advantage of the support and resources available to them. Motivation will dramatically increase if they can come to their realization by applying the science presented in the last couple of chapters to their situation.

Chapter 5: The Biological Injury Analogy

A running back in football gets the handoff. He runs through the hole created by the offensive line. Out of nowhere, the safety comes up and hits the running back in the leg. Due to the angle of the leg and the velocity of the safety's tackle, the running back experiences a severe fracture of his femur or thigh bone. X-rays and MRIs show that the running back suffered a significant biological injury.

> What expectations do we put on the running back?
>
> Would we expect him to get back in the game during the next series of downs?
>
> Would we expect him to play the next game or the rest of the season?
>
> How does the fan base view the running back?
>
> Do they call him lazy or a drain on the salary cap if he does not play for several games?

The running back experienced a biological injury due to an event that was out of his control. Most people understand that he would need time and resources to heal fully. Now, let's examine how this contrasts to someone experiencing the biological injuries associated with trauma.

Trauma, especially complex trauma, makes it difficult to regulate one's emotions and focus on tasks, and makes it challenging to create and maintain healthy relationships. Just as the running back's injury makes walking without crutches difficult, if not impossible, trauma makes it difficult for many to succeed in school, employment, or relationships.

No one would blame the running back for using crutches and walking with a limp. However, many in our society who do not understand trauma feel like those struggling with the biological injury of trauma are unmotivated or in some other way defective, and have little value to society. Why do we judge a biological injury to a leg bone so differently than a biological injury to the brain?

Let's think about the running back again. The running back is still financially supported while receiving the care, support, and resources needed to heal the leg injury. He goes through surgery, attends physical therapy, and starts to integrate back into practices slowly. As long as he is following medical treatment protocols, no one is calling him unmotivated or lazy for taking the time he needs to heal fully.

As with a broken bone, the biological injuries of trauma also heal with the right mix of treatment, support, and resources. Safe places to live, mental-health and substance-abuse treatment, medical care, supportive friends and family, and resources to help ensure economic stability can heal the damage done by traumatic experiences. With the right mix of motivation, resources, and support, those with traumatic pasts restructure their lives, and with hard work, achieve their dreams.

There is another critical similarity to the biological injuries of the running back's leg and the brain of someone experiencing trauma. The timing of the treatment and support is crucial. Imagine the difference in the recovery process for a running back who gets treatment right away and one that gets no treatment at all for several years. First, the player that does not get immediate treatment will suffer for years with the pain and disability of his injured leg. Second, when treatment happens, it will likely take longer for the running back to get back on the field, as work now has to focus on the original injury and the damage done in the several years since the original injury.

The biological injury of trauma and treatment have a similar relationship. Treatment is most effective when provided soon after the traumatic event. While delayed treatment is still highly effective, it will take longer to heal. If additional trauma happened since the initial incident, it is likely that the person will need more intensive treatment to heal the injuries and turn the trauma into increased resiliency and wisdom.

> Why do you think we look at physical injuries to other parts of the body differently from injuries from trauma to the brain?
>
> Why do you think society judges people with neurobiological injuries differently from athletes with other types of physical injuries?
>
> What treatments, support, resources, and hard work do you think people with traumatic pasts need to heal and

recover from their injuries and to live the lives they desire for themselves?

Matt's Notes

This analogy is a powerful one. I usually present it after providing some of the neurobiological research provided in the previous chapters. Doing so allows me to go into more depth on the biological or neurobiological injuries of trauma.

This analogy makes for a great group discussion. I suggest pausing after the initial questions for discussion and reflection. This opportunity helps people to think differently about how they view themselves and their past behaviors. This shift is a crucial goal of this analogy.

The other goal in presenting trauma in this light is to help people understand that with the right mix of support, resources, and motivation, they can heal from their pasts and break out of the prison of trauma. This insight will provide you with a wealth of change talk and allow you to implement MI techniques to explore this talk in more detail, while identifying ambivalence and building motivation for change.

The short nature of this analogy makes it useful in a variety of settings. If you present any of the research in the previous chapter, you can add it as a way to destigmatize trauma and put healing in a practical context. I also find this analogy extremely useful in my advocacy work. The analogy of the running back brings the science of trauma to life, helping people understand the reasons behind many of the struggles our clients face.

Chapter 6: The Cup Analogy

The cup analogy is a simple way to understand how stress and trauma affect our thoughts, feelings, and behaviors. The analogy has two parts; the first is the size of the cup. The bigger the size of the cup, the more stress we can experience while remaining in our prefrontal cortex or thinking part of our brain.

Factors such as living a healthy life, building self-confidence in one's skills and abilities, having healthy relationships, practicing mindfulness, following healthy diets, age, and utilizing an exercise program increase the size of our cup. Conversely, a poor diet, stress from poverty and financial problems, unresolved trauma, certain traumatic brain injuries, drug abuse, struggles with employment or at school, and being in unhealthy relationships decrease the size of our cup. Typically, the capacity of our cup stays consistent over time if we do not experience major life changes. The exception to this rule is trauma, which reduces capacity quickly, and if healing does not occur, can keep capacity low over long periods of time (Siegel, 2007; Siegel, 2011).

The second component of this analogy concerns the water in the cup. The water represents stress in our body at any given time. The experience of stress is a result of two chemicals, cortisol and epinephrine.

Cortisol is a chemical that prepares our bodies for physical activity. Throughout human history, stressful situations required a physical response, giving us the strength to either run away from a predator or to fight an enemy; this is the fight or flight response. Cortisol shifts the fuel of the brain, oxygen and glucose, or the blood sugar we get from food, toward the muscles in our arms and legs and away from our brain, preparing us for action (Siegel, 2007).

Epinephrine, or adrenaline, is a chemical that intensifies the cortisol reaction, giving us even more energy and strength. Epinephrine is not always released when a person feels stressed. Only when the event becomes increasingly stressful, which happens during most traumatic experiences, will the brain release epinephrine so that our response matches the intensity of the situation. When epinephrine is released, the cup will fill up almost immediately (Pierce, 2006).

As a cup fills, we start to lose our capacity for cognitive functioning and emotional regulation, as energy goes from the thinking parts of the brain to the emotional and reactive parts. As the water reaches the top of our cup, we go into crisis and operate in full survival mode. When this happens, we lose the ability to engage with other people effectively, to logically choose the right words or behaviors for the situation, or to consider the long-term consequences of our actions.

> Take a deep breath and check in on how your body feels. How full is your cup right now?

> Take a moment to think about the stress in your cup right now. What are some things that are adding stress to your cup?
>
> Can you recognize any stress, frustration, or embarrassment that you are carrying around from events that happened hours or days ago?

Stress accumulates in our cups over time. In other words, if we don't do things to get stress out of our cups, we carry it with us. This accumulated stress fills our cups up over time. Sometimes behaviors resulting from full cups are not just due to our present situation, but result from the stress we have experienced over the course of the day or several days.

Another concept that will help us understand how stress affects our thinking and behaviors is the window of tolerance. You can think about the space between the top of your cup and the level of water in your cup as your window of tolerance (Ogden, Minton, & Pain, 2006). When we have adequate space between the level of water in our cup and the top, we can say that we are in our window of tolerance and our thinking is flexible, adaptive, coherent, energized, and stable, or FACES for short. FACES is an important acronym to remember. If FACES describes your thinking and behaviors, you are operating from your prefrontal cortex, the thinking and planning part of the brain (Siegel, 2011).

Hyperarousal Zone (Flight/Fight): Increased sensation; emotional reactivity; hypervigilance; disorganized cognitive processing

	Rigidity	Chaos
↕	Window of Tolerance: Flexible; adaptive; coherent; energized; stable	
	Rigidity	Chaos

Hypoarousal Zone (Freeze): Relative absence of sensation; numbing of emotions; disabled cognitive processing; reduction of physical energy

When your stress level starts to fill up your capacity, your thinking and behaviors become rigid or chaotic. These responses are a final effort to control the stressful situation before going into crisis. Some people react to stress by trying to organize and control their world, which indicates a rigid response (Siegel, 2016).

When we apply the rigid response, we might start bossing people around or putting unrealistic expectations on ourselves or others. We might also feel a great deal of anxiety or sadness when things frustrate us and don't go exactly how we want them to go. Still another rigid response is obsessing over something, even if it is not that important. When we are rigid, it is hard to think creatively and we often automatically rely on behaviors we used in the past, even if they have had negative consequences.

> Can you identify a time when your behavior or thinking was rigid?

> How did your thinking and resulting behaviors affect you or others?

The chaos response is a reaction designed to create distance between us and what is filling up our cup with stress. We often achieve this distance by yelling, threatening, or using intimidating behaviors or words. Unfortunately, we often say things that hurt others and get us in trouble. Even though we are just trying to get space, others experience our behavior as dangerous and disrespectful (Siegel, 2011).

> Can you identify a time when your thinking became chaotic?
>
> How did your thinking and behavior affect you or others?

If rigidity or chaos does not alleviate the stress, our cup overflows and we are in crisis. In crisis or survival mode, we will rely on one of three reactive behaviors. The specific survival behavior will differ for every person and each unique situation. For most of us, there is a sequential pattern of survival reactions that have developed throughout human evolution.

The initial responses are to mobilize energy toward action: the hyperarousal response. The hyperarousal response that gets activated first in most situations is the flight response. The flight response directs energy into escaping the threat and putting as much distance as possible between us and the stress filling up our cup. In flight mode, we will reactively try to escape the situation at all costs. Think about the early history of humans. If we saw a saber-toothed tiger and the tiger did not see us, our best chance for survival was to get as far away from the tiger as possible; this is the flight response (Ogden, Minton, & Pain, 2006).

If it is not feasible to escape the stress, energy is then mobilized to fight against whatever is causing the stress. Fight is a hyperarousal response that can manifest in verbal or physical aggression. If we cannot escape the tiger, we must stand and fight with all our might. Like the flight response, the fight response leaves us with little or no ability to engage with the environment intellectually. In many cases, we strike out verbally or even physically at the person or thing causing the stress (Ogden, Minton, & Pain, 2006).

The third response is the hypoarousal or freeze response. If the flight or fight responses fail, the last option is to shut down. In this reaction, blood pressure drops, heart rate and breathing slow, and sensations and emotions numb. The freeze response occurs when we feel that we cannot flee or fight back. The tiger has us pinned down, making escape impossible.

Freeze can also be the default response for those of us who have experienced repeated physical or sexual abuse. In these situations, we had little physical, social, or economic opportunity or power to flee or fight back. The only way we survived is by shutting down, and in extreme cases, dissociating from the situation to survive physically and psychologically. Dissociation means that we mentally disconnect from reality. If you have ever forgotten an event or felt like you were outside your body watching from a distance, you may have dissociated (Ogden, Minton, & Pain, 2006).

Can you identify a time in the past when you experienced the fight, flight, or freeze responses?

What happened when you engaged in these responses?

How did it feel to be outside your window of tolerance?

The window of tolerance provides a model to help us understand our stress behaviors as natural, rather than as oppositional or bad. The critical thing to remember is that the hyper- and hypo-aroused states are reactions to things in our environment and are not a reflection of our overall personality or value as a human being. Unfortunately, when threats appear everywhere, living outside the window of tolerance can become a way of life.

Use the cup analogy to ask yourself throughout the day how much stress is in your cup right now? If you feel like it is getting full, have some strategies to help you regulate the stress in your cup. Some good coping activities are taking deep breaths, going for a walk in a park or performing some other physical activity, and talking to someone about what is stressing you out. The goal is to take positive action before your cup starts to overflow.

Matt's Notes

I love the cup analogy! Whether I'm talking to clients or training staff, it sticks with people. I often have people come up to me at conferences years after attending one of my training and saying, "We still talk about cups every day!"

The cup analogy provides clients with insight into their emotions and behaviors. A client who cannot say, "I'm starting to feel stressed and might explode soon if you keep making me fill out this paperwork" can utilize this analogy to simply communicate, "My cup is pretty full right now."

Cups are also useful at the beginning of the conversation. Early on, I ask the question, "How full is your cup today?" If a client communicates that their cup is full, I know that I need to spend some time up front letting them talk about their stress. Talking about stress gets it out of our cup. Our language has sayings to describe this experience, such as "getting it off your chest" or "feeling like something lifted off your shoulders."

The cup analogy grew my compassion and empathy for clients who are facing countless stressors in their lives. Many clients start their interactions with us with cups full from threats of violence, eviction notices, poverty, addiction, and other intense stressors. About 90 to 95% of the time when I asked, "How full is your cup today?" I got back the answer, "Full." Instead of jumping to items on my agenda for our meeting, a few minutes of processing their stress gave me crucial insight into their situation, while opening up their window of tolerance so I could work with their cognitive brain.

Part 3: Talking about Change

The book contains numerous strategies for helping clients consider and realize life changes. Part III: Talking about Change is designed to help teach clients about their change by presenting analogies and models to bring the change process to life. All of the strategies in Part III are intended for implementation in alignment with the spirit of MI and the communication approaches and strategies on eliciting change talk that are presented in the book.

The goal of this part is to help clients gain insight into their change, struggles, and condition through psycho-educational content. Knowledge is power, and knowing oneself elicits greater motivation and momentum for meaningful change.

Chapter 7: Elephant and Rider

The human brain is amazing and complex. Our brains require a great deal of energy to operate; the brain creates habits to save time and run more efficiently. It takes much less energy to repeat a habit the brain has done every day for years than to engage in a new and novel behavior. While brains are great at repeating habits over and over, they are not so good at trying to break habits with change behaviors.

Changing behaviors, thinking, or emotional responses to situations requires a tremendous amount of energy exertion from the emotional and intellectual parts of the brain. We do not make meaningful change without effectively engaging in the process both intellectually and emotionally. However, these same parts of the brain are structured in a way to support old behaviors and they will struggle to consider and accomplish significant changes.

To help us understand the complex science behind change, we will use an analogy of an elephant and rider put forth by psychologist Jonathan Haidt (2006). Dr. Haidt's analogy beautifully illustrates the interaction between the intellectual and the emotional brain when it comes to making difficult changes or breaking free of addictions. In Dr. Haidt's analogy, the rider represents the thinking brain and the elephant represents the brain areas associated with feelings and emotions. To make a successful change, we must get both the rider and elephant from their current location, describing our current way of thinking or habits, to a new destination, where we adopt new ways of thinking and healthier behaviors.

At first glance, the rider seems in total control. The rider sits on top with the best view and holds the reins. However, the rider's power over the elephant is precarious at best. While well positioned, if the 11,000-pound elephant wants to go in a particular direction, the rider is along for the trip with little or no power to influence where the elephant is going.

Our brains operate in much the same way. Emotions such as fear, terror, embarrassment, suffering, desire, and insecurity quickly override our thinking brain. When emotional, we often act irrationally and chaotically. When the emotional brain is in control, we are more likely to rely on old behaviors as coping skills, even if our rational brain understands that these actions are harmful.

The elephant relies on instinct and chooses short-term gratification by avoiding pain and seeking pleasure. Unfortunately, change requires us to delay gratification. We turn down the immediate pleasure of a glass of whiskey or bowl of cookie-dough ice cream for the long-term benefits to our sobriety and health. The elephant wants immediate payoffs, struggling to see any benefits in delaying the experience of pleasure (Heath & Heath, 2010).

Elephants get spooked easy. Most changes require that we give up something that we get some pleasure from or that helps us reduce pain in our lives. Just thinking about this loss might elicit feelings of fear, panic, and uncertainty. Change also means that we face the consequences of our old behaviors. Owning up to our pasts brings up feelings of shame, guilt, and embarrassment. The elephant struggles to remain calm when confronted with the emotional aspects of a difficult change. Too often these emotions cause the elephant to run away, argue vehemently against someone helping them with their change, or feel overwhelmed and just freeze in place, losing any motivation for action.

While elephants get the blame for many failed change attempts, riders also get us in trouble. Riders tend to overthink and obsess over the smallest details. If the rider engages in this rigid type of thinking, both the rider and elephant will just sit still and go nowhere. The rider can become so concerned with the first step that the elephant will get tired and just lay down.

While the rider and elephant both have their weaknesses, they also have strengths that are critical to change. The elephant provides the motivation and energy to tackle our change and get from our current location to our desired one. Think about your future five years from now, if you are successful in making all the changes you want to in your life. What emotions do you feel? These emotions are the fuel for the journey and pull the elephant toward that future (Haidt, 2006).

The elephant is also motivated to get away from emotions associated with harmful consequences connected to your current situation. Many of our behaviors negatively affect our health, financial standing, or ability to live the life we want for ourselves and our families. The emotions you feel when you answer the question, "If you continue down the path you are currently on, what would your life look like ten years from now?" can push the elephant toward a better future, if it does not feel overwhelmed. Regardless if the elephant is pushed or pulled by emotions, it moves in a positive direction (Rock, 2009).

The rider provides direction through strategic thinking and planning future steps. When the elephant is motivated to move in a positive direction, the rider's job is to implement a strategy to arrive successfully at the correct destination. Elephants can easily get lost if the rider does not guide them.

A skilled rider, or a mindful and robustly thinking brain, knows when to take control. A rider can recognize when the elephant is getting nervous or fearful and can calm it down to keep it on the right path. Use coping skills, mindfulness, and reassuring self-talk, a rider holds the elephant's focus and prevents it from running off into old habits or ways of thinking.

Think about a future where you have successfully made the changes you wish to make in your life.

> What does this future look like?
>
> How does it differ from the present?
>
> When you envision this future, how does it make you feel?

Think about the future consequences if you are unable to make these changes.

> What about this future motivates you to act?

How does this future compare to a future where you were able to make changes?

Take some time to think about the journey from your present situation into your desired future.

What are some very small steps you can take today to move in a positive direction toward the future?

What resources would you need to help you reach your desired future?

Whose support do you need to reach your desired future?

Matt's Notes

The elephant and rider analogy is incredibly effective in helping clients view change as both an emotional and cognitive process. You can expand client's understanding by bringing in the neurobiology material from previous chapters. As you probably understood, the elephant is the amygdala and sympathetic nervous system, and the rider is the cortex and prefrontal cortex.

If you have taught the cup analogy, it is also a useful tool for getting clients to think about how stress affects the rider's ability to control the elephant's behavior. When the cup is full, the rider might get very rigid and try to control the environment to manage stress. If this is unsuccessful, the elephant's reactive, chaotic, and instinctual side gains more control, leading to fight, flight, or freeze responses.

The questions at the end are powerful ones, and I caution you not to go through them all at once. Instead, introduce the concept of elephant and rider and the questions around envisioning a desired future. Only then should you tackle the questions concerning consequences, if you think they would be helpful.

This approach is strategic. The pull motivation created by envisioning the desired future is where the change talk and desire will come forth. The push motivation will elicit change talk on reasons and need. We want to start with the positive, because the worst-case question can spook the elephant. Visualize the push motivation created by the worst-case question as a gentle pat on the elephant's backside. We want to avoid having it feel like a hard smack in the butt, because the elephant might kick back!

The final set of questions about the journey are designed to engage the rider. View these questions as an assessment of where the client is in their stages of change, as a potential opportunity to establish a shared agenda, and when ready, to create a detailed concrete plan. The answer to the question will show where the client is in the early stages and their thinking about change.

The more detailed and long-term a client's answers, the more likely they are to be in the preparation stage. If you clearly identify this level of thinking, then it is okay to get more detailed and concrete. Ensure you do not try to force a premature focus on the client, as resistance is likely and the client might miss the valuable lessons of the analogy.

Chapter 8: Teaching the Stages of Change

Previously, many scientists believed that our personality and the brain were not flexible beyond the first few years of life. Advancements in brain-scanning technology show that this is not true. We now know that your brain is continually changing. The ability of the brain to change is called neuroplasticity; this shows how brain structure evolves to incorporate new behavior, ways of thinking, emotional states, and experiences (Schwartz & Begley, 2002).

While the brain is plastic and flexible, the same science shows us why change is so difficult. The brain is always looking to save energy; it does this by forming habits. Repeated behaviors, feelings, or thoughts create stronger connections between the brain cells, or neurons, associated with the behavior, feeling, or thought. These connections form pathways that make it easier to repeat the behavior in the future. Every time an action happens, the bonds strengthen, and it takes less overall energy to activate the next time. Changing behaviors, lifestyles, and ways of thinking is so difficult because it requires changing the physical brain in ways that support the new actions and thinking.

Envision the creation of a new habit as a trail through a forest. The first time a person walks in a particular direction in the woods, it is slow and arduous, many obstacles are present, and it is easy to get lost without a trail to follow. Each time another person takes the same path, it becomes more visible and easier to travel. Some paths become trails, and if these trails become used frequently, they might even get paved, making them accessible to faster modes of travel, such as bicycles and cars.

In this analogy, the forest represents our brain and the poorly marked and hard-to-follow trail represents a new behavior or way of thinking. The paved roads are representing our habits and the strong pathways in our brains that support that behavior. When you wake up on any given day, your brain is ready to go down the highly traveled road and, unless you are mindfully considering a new choice, will not even consider traveling down the more difficult trail.

Habits are ideal for saving energy, although unfortunately many compromise health and well-being. Changing a habit requires weakening the roads or pathways in the brain that support it. At the same time, consciously choosing to engage in healthier behaviors starts creating new brain structures. Which is more efficient: traveling the highway or hiking through a forest with no trail? Changing behavior means changing the actual physical structure of the brain. This rewiring takes time and happens in stages (Siegel, 2011).

The stages-of-change model is a great way to think about your change and the essential steps you can take to replace harmful or unproductive habits with healthy new ones. Let's take a moment to review each of the stages. As we do, think about a change you have successfully made in the past and one you are considering making in the next few weeks.

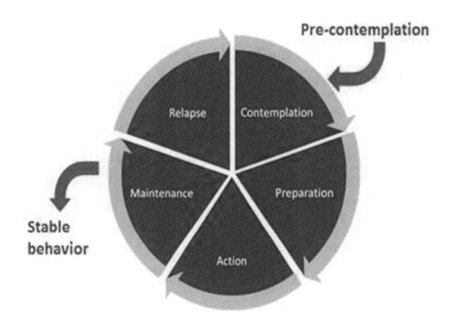

Pre-contemplation

Do you know someone who cannot see how their behaviors are hurting them or those around them, and this prevents them from living the life you want them to live? You might have tried to convince them that they should change, but you got nowhere. Instead of seeing your logic, maybe they became angry in a way that damaged your relationship with them.

At the beginning of the change journey, there is no motivation or even recognition that change is needed. People who care about us often realize that our behaviors and habits are hurting us before we recognize the damage we are doing to ourselves. This lack of conscious acknowledgment that change is needed characterizes the pre-contemplation stage. In this stage, we lack any desire to change and have not seen any reason or need even to consider it seriously.

Our challenge in pre-contemplation is to listen to others when they give us feedback. The ability to reflect and contemplate how our behaviors are hurting ourselves or others is a difficult task. It is natural in the early stages to get angry or defensive when others give us tough feedback. It takes a great deal of strength to take this feedback seriously and consider if a change is needed.

We can build upon the trail analogy presented earlier to demonstrate how pathways of brain cells strengthen and weaken over time. Here our trail forks off in two different directions. The habit we are trying to change, let's say smoking, forks to the left. We have smoked at least a pack a day for the last ten years. The pleasure resulting from epinephrine and dopamine associated with the nicotine reinforces the strength of the left trail. Over the years, the path to the left has become a superhighway, as smoking is a regular part of our lives.

The road to the right leads to quitting smoking. It is barely visible or nonexistent when we are in the pre-contemplation stage. Our brain is saving energy by repeating what we did yesterday and the day before, without any conscious consideration that the behavior might be harmful. Each time we smoke, it reinforces the smoking road, making it more efficient to be traveled again in the future. It is possible that we could go through the entire day and smoke a whole pack of cigarettes without ever thinking once about our desire for the next cigarette or the negative consequence of smoking. Our brains become very good at supporting our habits or addictions without entertaining any thoughts about stopping.

Here are some questions to help identify any possible changes that are in the pre-contemplation stage:

> Can you think of any changes that others encouraged you to make but that you excused as being unimportant?

> Are there any behaviors or habits that you know are harming you but that you do not even want to think about quitting because it seems too hard or overwhelming?

> Think about a successful change you made at some point in your life; can you remember how you were thinking and feeling in the pre-contemplation stage?

Contemplation

Before we begin this section on the contemplation stage, please take a moment to answer the following about a change you are considering:

> On a scale of 1 to 10 (1 being not at all important and 10 being extremely important), how important is it for you to change?

There is a moment of truth. Someone we respect gives us some hard feedback, our health takes a turn for the worse, or we suffer a severe consequence to our behavior such as an arrest or overdose. In pre-contemplation, we are unable to see how our situation affects our life and health. Once we get powerful feedback that shows us a behavior is harmful, we move out of the unconscious pre-contemplation stage to the contemplation stage.

In the contemplation stage, we, often reluctantly, acknowledge that a problem exists. For many of us, this insight carries with it elevated levels of anxiety, shame, and guilt. If strong enough, this emotional reaction becomes denial and pushes us back into pre-contemplation.

Let's return to the smoking example. Maybe we got some news from our doctor about how our smoking is affecting our health or we noticed that we are coughing more and even going upstairs makes us lose our breath. Contemplation is the stage where we start changing the brain to support a new behavior. Thinking seriously about a change begins the first journey down the new trail, as our brain adapts to new ways of thinking, even if we have taken no action.

As new pathways form, the old stronger pathways still win the day as we continue to engage in old habits through the contemplation stage. The ingrained behavior and pathways are too strong and the new connections are too weak to result in immediate behavioral change. However, even though the behavior doesn't change, the road supporting change strengthens every time we contemplate the change (Miller & Rollnick, 2012). There are two critical tasks in the contemplation stage: identifying ambivalence and confronting our discrepancies.

Identifying Ambivalence

Ambivalence is wanting more than one thing, even though the desires are incompatible with one another. Ambivalence keeps us locked into harmful behaviors or habits. The step of identifying our type of ambivalence provides us with a foundation to guide our contemplation of change (Miller & Rollnick, 2012).

The first type of ambivalence is approach/approach. This ambivalence occurs when we struggle with two choices that both have positive outcomes. Considering one option accentuates the attractiveness of the other and vice versa. While approach/approach can delay decision making, it is usually the least stressful form of ambivalence. The good thing about approach/approach is that it does not keep us stuck in the contemplation stage for long (Miller & Rollnick, 2012).

> Can you identify a choice between two options you struggled with lately because both would bring you something good?

The second type of ambivalence is avoidance/avoidance. Here the choice is between two unpleasant alternatives. Avoidance/avoidance is the old situation of being stuck between a rock and a hard place. As we move toward deciding on one option, the negatives of that choice become more evident, and the alternative might begin to look more favorable. Unfortunately, as soon as we move toward the alternative, the negatives of that decision come into focus (Miller & Rollnick, 2012).

> Can you identify a choice you struggled with lately because both had strong negative or unpleasant consequences or outcomes?

While the first two types of ambivalence concern choice, the next two can also refer to changes we are considering. The third type of ambivalence is approach/avoidance. In approach/avoidance, the change we are weighing has both strong positive and negative aspects. When we contemplate acting to realize the change, the negatives become more apparent, and we lose motivation. Loss of motivation leads to inaction, resulting in a feeling of anxiousness because we are not getting the positive aspects that would come with the change (Miller & Rollnick, 2012).

Hard changes and choices are difficult because we must give up or do something that feels uncomfortable. Quitting smoking has tremendous health and financial benefits, and contemplating these rewards increases our motivation for change. As that motivation moves us to act, we might experience or fear nicotine withdrawal. In our smoking example, long-term rewards of more money and health are fighting against our instincts to enjoy the pleasures of smoking and avoid the pain of withdrawal.

> Can you identify a change you struggled with lately because of conflicting positive and negative consequences?

The final type of ambivalence is double approach/avoidance. Here we confront two potential options, each of which has both positive and negative aspects. Considering one choice makes the negative dimensions of that decision more prominent, while enhancing the positive aspects of the other option. Moving toward the second option, however, makes its negatives more apparent, while making the first choice seem more attractive (Miller & Rollnick, 2012).

Double approach/avoidance is very common when we are considering significant life changes. These changes usually require a series of double approach/avoidance choices. In contemplation stage, it is essential that we consider the decision logically. Often our emotional reactions to the negative aspects of a change keep us from moving toward action. Labeling your ambivalence is an intellectual exercise that permits us to engage the thinking part of our brain in our decision making without getting overwhelmed by our emotions.

> Can you identify any approach/avoidance ambivalence in the change you are considering?

Confronting Our Discrepancies

Discrepancies are the differences between the life we desire and the current reality. As we identify our ambivalence, we are naming our reasons to stay the same and our reasons for change. When we confront discrepancies, we examine how our current behavior and thinking is preventing us from living a life we desire for ourselves and our family.

To confront our discrepancies, we must first identify the values or rules that guide our choices and behaviors. Our values are core to who we are as people. The better our behaviors align with our values, the better our mental health and well-being.

When our lives are out of line with what we value most, it can result in considerable anxiety (Achor, 2010; Rock, 2009).

Take a moment to answer these each of these questions.

> Tell me what you care most about in life. What matters most to you?
>
> What would you say are the rules you live by?

Now think about your change again and answer these two questions:

> How does your current behavior contradict your values?
>
> How would changing your behavior allow you to align your life with your values better?

How do you feel after this exercise? When we realize that our behavior deviates from our values, it creates anxiety. While this anxiety feels uncomfortable, it pushes us to change our behaviors so that we can relieve the tension. The good thing about this anxiety is that it can turn into motivation. Values help us identify three key drivers that determine whether we are successful in making our change.

The drivers are our desire, reason, and need to make the change. Desire is the extent to which we want the change to happen. Reason speaks to why we are considering the change. Need is the importance and urgency that push us to consider the change; need often involves external consequences that will happen if we fail to make the change (Miller & Rollnick, 2012).

Next let's take a moment to reflect on your desire, reason, and need concerning your change. Please answer the following for each that apply:

> What desire do you have to make this change?
>
> What reasons can you identify that make this change important?
>
> Why do you need to make this change?

Now think about your answer to the importance-ruler question:

> On a scale of 1 to 10 (1 being not at all important and 10 being extremely important), how important is it for you to change?
>
> Has the number shifted in any way? Why do you think it changed or stayed the same?

Preparation

Before beginning this section, please answer the following question:

> On a scale from 1 to 10 (1 being not at all confident and 10 being extremely confident), how confident are you that you could make this change?

The preparation stage involves us identifying the best strategy to successfully make our change and having the self-confidence to implement our plan. Other people are essential throughout the stages of change, as they give us feedback, listen, and support us in our contemplation. In preparation for change, other people will help us create the best strategy possible, provide us with feedback, and identify barriers or opportunities we might be missing because of our emotional investment in both the positive and negative outcomes of the change.

When we envision taking action on a plan for change, we are reinforcing the trail first created in the contemplation stage. Planning engages the mind and empowers it to over-ride the habits and instinctual responses of the brain. As Alan Lakein (1973) stated,

Control begins with Planning. Planning is bringing the future into the present so that you can do something about it now.

In our smoking example, we might start gathering information on patches, gum, support groups, and other resources that we could utilize to help us quit. Maybe we could talk to a friend who stopped smoking to learn from their experience. We have not taken actions to quit smoking, but we are gathering information, support, and resources to reinforce action when we are ready.

Just as our desire, reason, and need for change move us from contemplation to preparation, our self-efficacy, or the belief in our ability to realize the change, moves us from preparation to action. Too many of us struggle to find confidence and self-efficacy when preparing for a significant life change. However, all of us have a set of strengths that can be positioned to build our self-efficacy and fuel our journey through the stages.

At the heart of self-efficacy are the strengths that you possess. Sometimes life makes us focus too much on our weaknesses and shortcomings; this focus destroys our self-efficacy and keeps us from moving to the action stage. Think about your change again and answer these three questions:

> What five changes have you made in your life that were difficult for you?
>
> What five personal strengths did you utilize to make these changes in the past?
>
> Given what you know about yourself, how could you use these strengths to make this new change successfully?

Take a moment to reflect on your answers and strengths.

> How did thinking about your strengths influence your perception of the change?

Finally, let's return to the confidence question and answer:

> On a scale from 1 to 10 (1 being not at all confident and 10 being extremely confident), how confident are you that you could make this change?
>
> Has your number changed? Why do you think it changed or stayed the same?

Action

The next stage is the action stage. In this stage, we implement our plan and begin to modify behaviors that support us in reaching our goals. In the action stage, people around us will start noticing the change. People who support us will celebrate these changes. Others who might still be engaging in our old habits, such as drug use, might unconsciously try to pull us back into unhealthy habits. Often, major life changes mean significant changes to our social group; for some of us this means saying goodbye to old friends and making new ones.

The action stage is one of starts and stops. We will often have conflicting feelings as we start to lose things we like about the old behavior, and we might experience adverse withdrawal or side effects from the change. For many, the change we are trying to make is one of the most challenging things we have ever attempted in our lives. The action stage tests our strengths as we struggle with past failures and feelings of self-doubt.

One of your most essential tasks in moving from the action stage to the maintenance stage is celebrating all positive steps in the change process. Even if the process is slower than we wish or we fall back into old behavior, we need to celebrate the accomplishments we do achieve. Trying to not smoke for a day, going to see a doctor about our medical condition, or reaching out to family members we have not seen in years can seem like relatively small accomplishments to an outsider, but are huge milestones for many of us (Miller & Rollnick, 2013).

Each celebration sends chemicals down the new trail; making it stronger reinforces our ability to repeat the positive behavior the next hour, day, and month. These chemicals, dopamine and serotonin, are like bulldozers for our new trail. When we do something that makes us feel good, we become motivated to repeat that behavior to feel good again. Celebrations reinforce brain changes, making us feel good and creating motivation to make the change permanent (Wagner & Harter, 2006).

Maintenance and Stable Behavior

The next phase is the maintenance stage and the stable-behavior stage. In these stages, the road supporting not smoking becomes the main thoroughfare. Smoking has stopped, and the new state of not smoking becomes the norm. Stable behavior occurs as the new behavior becomes hardwired and the old pathways lose strength. The mind can disengage to a certain extent at this point. Smoking is no longer a habit supported by the biology of the brain, as not smoking has become the norm.

Our brains might start to miss the benefits of the old behavior, such as the feeling of getting high or the people we used to hang around with who also engaged in the behavior we are eliminating. These feelings can tempt us back into old behaviors, as we will see in the relapse stage. Change can be like climbing a very high ladder. When the focus is solely on the climb, all we need to do is put one hand over the next. At some point, we have risen so high that we take a break and look around. Seeing how high we have climbed is a scary realization and can quickly overwhelm the self-efficacy we have worked so hard to build.

In the maintenance and stable-behavior stages, you may notice an increase in self-efficacy and start to consider additional life changes. The realization of some of the initial goals often requires revising the plan that was established in the preparation stage, as new opportunities and challenges become evident. Now that drug use is under control, people might ask us to consider going back to school or getting a job. These changes can bring up a whole new set of insecurities and fears. It is important to realize that progress through one change does not mean we can immediately jump to the action stage with a new change. In fact, starting from the contemplation stage helps set us up for success with the new challenge, while preventing relapse on our current change.

Relapse

Relapse can happen at any point in the stages of change. Relapse can be one of the toughest setbacks, as it feels like we have failed ourselves and others. It is essential to remember that relapse into old behavior is a normal part of the change process and is more likely than not to happen at some point.

When we relapse, it may be a brief glitch in our plan, or it may put us back into an earlier stage of change. Relapse often leads us to question if we even really want to change. Fear can creep in that the habit is stronger than we are.

Relapse is natural. Even though the old superhighways have turned into sidewalks, they still exist. The brain craves the high or positive experiences that the old habit provided. Sometimes this pull is too strong to resist, and the old biology wins the day. Other times, our brain, drawn by temptations or cravings, might intellectualize its way into relapse. "Just one cigarette won't hurt anything," or similar conscious thoughts can be as much to blame for relapse as the unconscious brain.

Self-confidence may erode, and hopelessness can sink in. When relapse has occurred, we often search for the reasons for the relapse. Sometimes we identify a strong unexpected urge or recognize that we let our guard down. Other times, relapse merely results from being tired, hungry, or frustrated with a person or situation, or because of some random event, such as running into someone with whom we used to get high.

Try not to view relapse as a failure. Instead, it is an opportunity to learn. Understand it as a part of the process of change and a signal that we might need to tweak our plan to address any triggers that might have led to the relapse. Most importantly, we need to focus on our accomplishments and successes in the action and maintenance stages more than the negative consequence of the relapse. If we obsess on the fact we relapsed, those brain structures that will pull us back into the behavior will get activated, and we'll repeat it. Make sure you focus on accomplishments and successes, as this will strengthen the brain structures associated with the new behaviors.

Here are some questions that help us focus our energy on getting back to the action and maintenance stages after a relapse:

> What positive results did you experience by getting to the action stage?
>
> How were you able to achieve this behavior change?
>
> How can you use the successes you achieved to avoid relapse in the future?

Matt's Notes

In this chapter, I combined aspects from the Mindsight chapter (Chapter 11) in the book into the stages of change. I did so to make the concepts more concrete and linear, and to support your implementation of MI strategies. The material presented in this chapter is excellent for group work, as it elicits change talk and helps the client realize that others also struggle to make change.

Throughout this process, make sure you are not the one making the argument for change. It might be helpful to revisit the resistance section in the Stages of Change chapter (Chapter 5) in the book. Remember, resistance occurs when you jump to a stage of change ahead of where the client is at that specific moment.

For a group format, you can start with an introduction to the stages of change. In this presentation, it's easier for most clients to think of someone else's change, as thinking about their change could sidetrack them from learning. At the end of the session, you can start having them considering a significant change they are trying to accomplish.

The second group session can focus on pre-contemplation. The real goal is, through a presentation of the material, to help them identify that they are in pre-contemplation and help them move to contemplation. While this will test the skills of even the most experienced group facilitator, having them identify changes that they wish friends or family would make, but recognizing that they are stuck in pre-contemplation, will help them turn the focus on themselves and consider changes others suggest they make.

Considering contemplation with ambivalence, values, and discrepancies could easily fill multiple group sessions. This topic will be especially helpful if group is the only psychosocial support the client is receiving. Whether in a group or through individual work, you want to make sure the client has adequate time to think through their ambivalence, identify values, confront discrepancies, and explore the resulting cognitive dissonance.

Preparation takes some thought, and most clients will need some individual help to create a logical and strategic plan for action. To set this stage for success, you might want to spend an entire group session on helping clients identify their strengths. Conversations about strengths and sharing with other group members are empowering.

In the preparation stage, we help the client work through creating shared agendas and then more formal planning, as outlined in the book. If the client is only engaged in group work, you'll want to give them time to process their plan, get feedback, and adjust. It helps many clients to process others' plans, as this gives them insights into their own plan. You can also have clients pair off and get support from fellow group members as they create their plans. If you do this, make sure you've established a sense of group safety and rules, as creating plans opens people up to vulnerabilities.

If you have a group of people in the early stages of change, you might want to do a group summarizing action, maintenance, and relapse. For those reaching action, you can spend more time exploring these stages. Regardless, make sure you spend significant time reinforcing that relapse is part of the process and not an outright failure. Time spent talking about relapse in this way will pay off big time when setbacks do happen.

Chapter 9: Social Networks and Change

Making a difficult change is often seen as a personal struggle. This struggle pits the person's willpower against the entrapments of their habits and addictions. Viewing change as a personal struggle is an outdated way to conceptualize behavioral change and improved health. Success depends on numerous factors all coming together with our motivation. The most powerful external factor in determining our success is the people in our lives.

Emotions and behaviors are contagious. Unconsciously, we take on many of the characteristics of those who surround us. If we spend most of our time with depressed people, we are likely to struggle with depression ourselves. If our family eats healthy food and we spend a great deal of time with them, we are likely to eat healthy as well (Christakis & Fowler, 2009).

We might like to think of ourselves as independent actors always making conscious decisions; in reality, we are a reflection of those around us. Author Jim Rohn (2010) sums up the science behind the influence of our social networks in his famous quote,

You're the average of the five people you spend the most time with.

If we are a reflection of the people we spend time with, how do you think this would influence your ability to make a successful life change? When we think about change, we think about what we can control and influence. When the focus is all internal, we might miss one of the most influential contributors to our success: the people in our lives.

Social-science research shows three levels of influence from our social networks. The first level of influence is the immediate relationships or people with whom you have frequent interactions. The second tier of influence comes from the people who are in relationships with these immediate relationships. Finally, the third level originates from the people in relationships with the people who are in relationships with your immediate relationships (Christakis & Fowler, 2009).

Whether researchers measure someone's chances of heart disease, smoking, or happiness, those with whom they regularly interact will increase that person's chances for that characteristic by around 15%. Now, this is where the research gets fascinating and maybe a little scary, depending on the social network. While our friends and family influence our behavior by around 15%, researchers also found that the family and friends of our immediate relations influence them, which in turn influences us by approximately 10%. Finally our friend's friend's friends and families influence us by approximately 7%. While these numbers fluctuate depending on what researchers measure, findings on many behaviors and emotions demonstrate that we live in the middle of a vast social network with enormous consequences to our health and well-being (Christakis & Fowler, 2009).

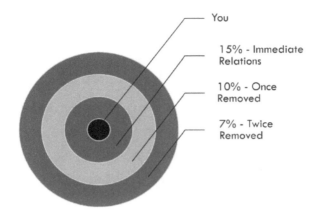

Let's use an example to demonstrate the concept as it relates to making a change of quitting smoking. In this case, we are going to say that a childhood friend named Jerry moves into town.

When you reconnect, you find that you and Jerry "click," just like you did when you were children. You start seeing Jerry weekly, if not more often, and Jerry becomes an immediate relationship in your network. Based on the research, whether or not Jerry smokes will strongly influence your ability to stop smoking.

If Jerry is a smoker, it hurts your chances of quitting. Why? For one, Jerry might offer you a cigarette, which could be difficult to turn down if you are trying to stop. Just being around the smell of cigarettes leads to cravings, making it more difficult not to smoke yourself. Jerry might also smoke after dinner or in the car, which is when you also enjoyed a cigarette. If he offers you one in these situations, you are much more likely to say yes.

On the other hand, if Jerry does not smoke, you are less likely to smoke when you hang out, and instead of smoking, you might pick up some of Jerry's hobbies or activities. If Jerry likes to go to baseball games, you might start liking baseball and following your home team. Jerry might enjoy riding bikes; it is likely he would ask you to join. As you can see, it is much more difficult to quit smoking around someone who smokes, and it is much easier when the person does other activities that do not involve smoking.

Emotions, behaviors, and habits are contagious. Surrounding ourselves with people struggling with similar harmful habits that we are trying to change makes changing incredibly difficult. Whether intentionally or unconsciously, those still engaging in these harmful habits will find it difficult to offer meaningful support and encouragement. It is difficult for someone to tell you how important it is for your health to quit smoking when they are holding a lit cigarette.

If we surround ourselves with people who do not engage in behaviors we are attempting to change, we maximize our chances of success. Support groups, Alcoholics Anonymous, and other groups of people who gather to support positive change are important factors in many people's change process. Others find great support in a friend or two who support them in the low moments and celebrate the accomplishments.

Let's take a moment to think about the influence of your social network.

> What are the top five emotions that you encounter in your normal week from those you hang out with most?
>
> What positive behaviors are you exposed to through your interactions with friends and family that support your change?
>
> What behaviors are you exposed to through your interactions with friends and family that might hurt your ability to change?

If you are currently in social networks that do not support your efforts to change, do not worry. Like other parts of the journey, making successful change relies on small actions implemented over time. Adjusting social networks does not mean you must disconnect from all your friends and family. It does challenge us to figure out ways to spend more time with people and groups who support our change. We might need to take breaks from certain people for a while during critical times in our change journey.

Let's think about this a little deeper.

> How can you strategically spend more time with people who support healthy behaviors and emotions that you want to adopt?
>
> What people or groups would increase your chances of successfully making your change?
>
> How can you minimize the influence of people who might hurt your ability to make your change a reality?

Matt's Notes

Social networks are an often-overlooked aspect of helping clients change. Even if you are the greatest MI guru in the world, if your client hangs out every day with people engaging in the behavior they are trying to change, their chances of making positive changes are minimal. Conversations concerning social networks are difficult at times, because they require reflection on the negative influences of families and friends. Just as with the other difficulties of change, these conversations are critical to success.

You can easily cover this material in one group or individual session. You can go deeper by having them map out their social networks and the emotional states and behaviors that those in their network expose them to on a regular basis. Family mapping is another way of showing the influence of family members on the client.

Regardless of the depth of exploration, the most critical element of this chapter is providing insight into the influence of others. Following up consistently on how others are affecting the client's ability to change is key, as it provides multiple opportunities to process the information throughout their stages of change. Finally, social networks provide you with the opportunity to talk about the importance of professional and peer support. This support could include mental health, substance abuse, a support group, AA or NA, connecting with a church, or other positive support systems.

Part 4: The Hero's Journey

Initially, I had planned to use the hero's journey to structure the entire book; however, the space needed to do it justice disrupted the flow of the book. Over the last couple of years, I have relied heavily on Joseph Campbell's concept of the hero's journey to structure my talks about trauma-informed care. I've always been pulled toward Campbell's research on mythology across diverse cultures, as it speaks about the human experience in a powerful way that connects us across geography and time. I read The Hero with a Thousand Faces (1949) in high school and have used it as a filter through which to view movies, current events, and popular culture ever since.

A few years ago, the music streaming service Spotify included days' worth of Campbell's lectures on their site. While many of these talks repeat common themes, I used it as an opportunity to dig deeper into his work and ways of thinking. It was after listening to about 30 hours of the recorded lectures that I was struck with a powerful realization.

While Campbell's focus was on religious and fictional heroes, I saw an interesting similarity between the journey he described and those of the clients I've worked with over the years. While he used mythical characters from Homer and religious scriptures, I saw my clients, their challenges, and the strengths they somehow accessed to overcome great hardship. As I sat through another 15 hours of lectures, I realized the hero's journey provided a perfect model for understanding the healing process, as clients move from trauma to post-traumatic growth.

This realization helped me with another struggle I was having in my trainings. At the time, I used a group activity where I have people consider the words "trauma victim" and what role trauma plays in the "victim's" life. Next, I have people consider the words "trauma survivor" and the role that trauma plays in the "survivor's" life. All groups eventually come to the same point – that a "victim" is under the control of their traumatic pasts and that the trauma is more powerful than their ability to cope. On the other hand, the survivor has become more powerful than the event and the resulting suffering. Their strength transcends the trauma, and they can bring this strength into other aspects of their life.

We then discuss the power of perception and how if someone sees themselves as a victim, they remain stuck in the victim mindset, but how those who view themselves as survivors transform pain and suffering into wisdom and strength. While this group activity made my point, I always struggled with the word "survivor." It didn't seem powerful enough to describe the intensity of the challenges and suffering my clients faced and eventually overcame. When I made the connection between Campbell's work and the process of realizing post-traumatic growth, I found the word I was looking for to describe a person who takes on the journey from trauma and suffering to strength and wisdom: Hero!

Imagine for a moment how our clients' lives would change if they could view themselves as a hero, or as someone who has experienced tremendous hardships, yet faces an opportunity to gain great strength and wisdom. They are heroes due to the difficulty of the journey, a journey that many people, unfortunately, do not survive. We, as a society, already stick various labels on those we work with: homeless, mentally ill, addicted, criminal, HIV-positive, abuser, unemployed, etc. Even if people work their way out of these labels, we often put on new labels that remind them of their past: recently released incarcerated is my current favorite—meaning I hate it!

What if, instead of seeing themselves as homeless, addicts, or criminals, they viewed their current struggles, traumas, and life situations as just part of a larger journey? I believe this does a couple of things. First, clients realize that the problem is not who they are, but a struggle to overcome; this supports the MI strategy of separating the person from the problem.

Second, the hero's journey shows the true scope of the challenge facing them due to their complex trauma history. Viewing the pain, suffering, and consequences of traumatic experiences as part of an epic journey and not as a permanent state is reassuring and empowering. Finally, understanding that the trauma and suffering are just the first part of their journey provides our clients and ourselves with a framework for recovery and growth that can help normalize the experience and spark the light of hope that is so critical to change.

As you read the following sections on the hero's journey, think about how you can integrate its structure into your individual or group interactions with clients. Through reflection, journaling, and conversations, clients can see themselves in a whole new light that transforms their personal narratives and unleashes great motivation for change. Let's begin our journey!

Chapter 10: Introduction to the Hero's Journey

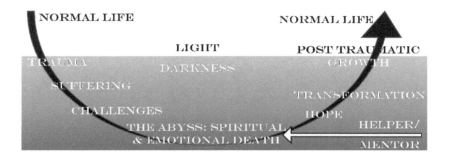

Trauma is a powerful and painful event in our life stories. It can isolate us, make us feel inferior, flood us with pain, and keep us stuck in destructive patterns of thoughts and behaviors. The pain of trauma can steal away a positive view of ourselves, relationships, and the world in which we live.

Anyone who experiences trauma is a victim of something. For those of us who have experienced abuse, violence, racism, assault, or betrayal, someone with physical, social, or economic power abused it and hurt us severely in the process. Others experience trauma as victims of a flood, hurricane, accident, or other human-made or natural disaster. Regardless, trauma by its very nature knocks us down and keeps us down for a time.

Some people can spend their entire lives feeling like a victim. These people live every day with the resulting pain and suffering of their traumatic experiences. This suffering becomes a prison that keeps them trapped, unable to live a happy and meaningful life. It is very easy to blame people in the victim mindset for not having the strength to just get over their suffering.

Blaming a victim is something we should avoid. Being trapped in the victim mindset has little to do with the personality of the person. Instead, it is the result of not getting the right mix of support, treatment, and resources they need to transform their pain and suffering into wisdom and strength. The good news is that there is hope for everyone to grow and recover from trauma.

To explore the transformative journey from pain and suffering to strength and wisdom, we will use a model based on the work of Joseph Campbell. Campbell studied mythology across different times and cultures. What he found is that our stories about heroes follow a similar pattern regardless of the century or location in which these stories took place.

Looking at Campbell's findings, we can see that his hero's journey describes the experience of those with traumatic pasts and the struggle to overcome pain and suffering. Any great story includes tremendous hardships and struggles. Heroes are not born heroes. Instead, heroes come forth when ordinary people find the strength and courage to face their pain and challenges, and find their true selves in the process. Let's start our examination of the hero's journey by reflecting on some heroes in our popular culture and what lessons they can teach us about our life journeys.

Think about the stories you read or your favorite movie growing up.

> Who were your childhood fictional heroes?
>
> What strengths did these heroes possess that made them great?
>
> What hardships faced your heroes and how did they overcome these obstacles?
>
> Who helped your hero? What role did these people or things play in your hero's journey?

Matt's Notes

The power of the hero's journey analogy is realized when we help change how our clients view themselves. The hope is that by the end of learning about the hero's journey, they transform their thinking about themselves and their situation. However, at the beginning of this journey, they are more likely to see strength in others than to identify it in themselves. Due to this, I suggest you have your client think about the strength they admire in heroes in popular culture. Movies and literature are a great starting place, because most authors use the hero's journey structure in their work.

Chapter 11: Descent into Darkness

The first step of the hero's journey is out of the light and security of ordinary life. For Campbell's heroes, there is a choice of whether or not to take their journey, as most have the option of staying home and continuing their normal life. Unfortunately, no one chooses to be sexually abused or assaulted, born into extreme poverty, or raised in a violent home. Instead of choice, a traumatic event forces us on the journey. There is no adventure here, no moral crisis, no glory sought.

While Campbell's heroes experience pain, trauma, grief, and suffering on their journeys, they do so in the context of adventure and search for self-discovery, and in the name of glory, wealth, and their god or gods. For those who experience trauma, the pain, grief, and suffering are a result of someone else choosing to inflict tremendous harm upon them. Even more tragically, this harm falls on a child or someone in a vulnerable position with less physical, economic, or social strength.

The experience of trauma forces the person to cross an invisible line between light and darkness. In any great book or movie, the crossing of this line is evident, as the tone and feel of the story changes in dramatic ways; trauma also dramatically changes our life story. Some people had "light" in our lives before the trauma in the form of a good home, economic stability, loving parents, or educational achievement. At some point, someone or something took away the light. For these people, the loss of light is a powerful and often overwhelming event, demonstrating trauma's power to destroy stability, peace, and hope.

Tragically, because of the early age that they experienced trauma, others never experienced light. Going back perhaps even to the moment of conception, stress, hardship, and pain characterized their lives. Research now shows that pregnant mothers can pass harmful chemicals in the womb to the developing fetus, either from drug use or stress hormones released during their mother's constant struggles with poverty, domestic violence, homelessness, and other stressful realities of her existence. These chemicals are passed from mother directly to the unborn baby during the most critical time in human biological development (Nakazawa, 2016).

Thanks to new animal and human research studies, we can now trace this passing of trauma to even before conception, all the way back to the formation of egg and sperm that created us (Wolynn, 2016; Yehuda et al., 2000; Yehuda et al., 2005; Yehuda et al., 2015). The egg that eventually created you developed inside your mother when your grandmother was five months pregnant with her. For a few months, three generations share the same biological environment. The traits that your grandmother needed to survive her stress and trauma were passed to your mother and, in a lesser but still significant way, to you (Finch & Loehlin, 1998).

Our father's sperm is affected differently. Sperm continues to multiply throughout life. Therefore, the makeup of sperm is affected by events that happen throughout the father's life, almost to the point of conception. The egg carries the history of your grandmother's trauma, the sperm reflects the more recent life experiences of your father, and then your mother passes on her experiences of the world while you are in the womb (Bale, 2015; Rudacille, 2011).

Through most of human history, the challenges of our parents and grandparents were likely to be our challenges as well. For many, this meant surviving violence, slavery, predators, poverty, hunger, and threats of disease. Expressing the traits that our ancestors used to survive their trauma helped us prepare for our life challenges (Hodge, 2014). It is also important to note that just because you are born to parents with traumatic histories does not mean that their biology is your destiny. Improving your environment, being surrounded by people who love you, economic security, experiencing success in academics or employment, and mental-health treatment can all help you experience different outcomes from your parents.

This passing of trauma from one generation to the next means we might have inherited some of our parents' and grandparents' pain and suffering. Once born, too many of us continued to experience stress and trauma due to the hardships of poverty, stressed or absent parents, and failing and violent neighborhoods and schools. Our genetics combined with stress and trauma affect how our brains develop and operate.

Luckily, brains are highly adaptive. They are always changing to give us the best chance to survive and thrive in the environments in which we live. If we grow up in stressful and dangerous situations, our young brain overdevelops the parts that help us survive. There is a cost to living in the darkness of poverty, homelessness, and violence. While the brain adapts to survive, it does so at the expense of the areas that help us succeed in the educational and employment environments so critical for economic and social health.

Technology allows us to observe how the darkness influences the biology of people living in traumatic situations. Campbell's hero goes into the darkness after knowing the security and safety of the light. Many of us survive the journey through homelessness, violence, and poverty without ever having a chance to experience the light. The unfortunate result for many of us is that we believe that life is pain and suffering, instead of these hardships being just temporary experiences in a more extensive journey.

The hero's journey transcends time. We carry the scars of our ancestors' suffering and hence risk passing on our pain to future generations. The compelling aspect of this science concerns our ability to transform and heal not only our pain, but trauma that hurt our ancestors. You face an amazing opportunity. If you find the courage to heal and transform your trauma, you not only heal the genetic scars of the past, you prevent your pain and suffering from passing on to future generations.

Matt's Notes

The goal of this chapter is to communicate the power of trauma. More so than other chapters in this part, you will want to customize this one for your client population. For those clients who would benefit from a thorough exploration of trauma, bring in the material from Chapter 3, Introducing Trauma and Neurobiology, and Chapter 6, The Cup Analogy. In other situations, you might want to shorten this chapter, speaking only to the client's experience and not exploring the research on intergenerational trauma.

The main point you want to explore is how trauma forced their life stories to change. There are two approaches you can utilize, depending on the goals and focus of your situation. For more therapeutic situations, you may want to spend a reasonable amount of time processing people's past traumatic experiences. This approach is effective in ongoing groups where there is already a high level of safety and trust among group members, or in your relationship with the client, if you are doing this in individual work.

Discussion questions for this approach could include:

> How do you see trauma affecting your life journey?
>
> What was your life like before you experienced trauma?
>
> What changed for you after the trauma?

The second, and safer, approach involves having clients focus on the heroes they identified in the previous chapter. Any great story involves trauma; you might want to focus more on fictional characters in movies or literature, since their trauma is often easier to identify than that of a sports hero or other popular culture figure. Here are some questions to structure discussions for this approach:

> Think about the hero in your favorite story or movie; what trauma did they experience?
>
> How did this traumatic experience change their lives and change the plot of the story or movie?
>
> How did the trauma impact the hero's personality and emotional state?

Chapter 12: Suffering, Challenges, and the Soul

We meet our hero in the darkness of trauma. The stress of the traumatic event has overwhelmed the person's biological, psychological, and social capacities, and the trauma and resulting anxiety have become the organizing factors of our hero's life. There is no safety or security, and little support; hope is, at best, a fading glimmer of light at the end of a long tunnel. Alone and lost, life becomes focused on surviving the pain. A world that has shown its evil and dark potential now dominates the horizon of our hero.

Phil Cousineau (2001), a student of Joseph Campbell, makes a statement that I found very insightful when talking about the experience of the hero's journey:

> I refer to this mystery as the difference between the 'overstory,' which is the visible plot, and the 'understory,' which is the invisible movement of the soul of the main characters. What is mysterious about mythic stories is how they always meander back to the same place: your soul. In this sense myth is a living force, like the telluric powers that stream through the Earth. It is this mythic vision, looking for the 'long story,' the timeless table, that helps us approach the deep

mysteries because it insists there is always more than meets the eye.

Using under- and overstory to represent suffering and challenges, respectively, pulls together both the internal experience of trauma, as well as the outward expressions of the hardships of pain and suffering. What connects the inward and outward for Cousineau is the soul, which others might also call the human mind. The hero's journey is not a journey of the body through physical space. Instead, the journey is one of the mind and soul from light into darkness and back to light.

Our overstory is what others see when they judge us without knowing our experiences. Too often people label us, and these labels put us into categories with those having similar struggles. When people label us, they miss our unique experience and overlook our strengths and resiliency. Many people could not survive a day in our shoes, yet are quick to judge us without getting to know our understories.

The understory of trauma is one of spiritual pain and, without help, the potential for spiritual death. Loss of the connection to spirit might be the best way to describe the darkness and internal experience of trauma. "Why did God, or another higher power, allow this to happen?" is a question that many must answer to ascend back into the light. Think about this question for a moment and the power it holds.

We don't need to go far in any sacred text to find the consequences of the separation of spirit or God. This absence represents darkness, and if there is light, it is usually the light of fire, commonly connected to damnation and unimaginable suffering. Trauma shakes our world and calls into question our faith or spirituality. Emerging from the darkness requires many of us to find a new and powerful connection to ourselves, others, and for many, spirit.

How do you think others who meet you perceive you? Attempt to write a brief overstory from the point of view of a stranger who meets you briefly on the street.

> What are people missing about you as a person when they just know your overstory?
>
> How has another's overstory about you affected how you see yourself and your understory?
>
> What would you like to change about your overstory?
>
> How would you like to rewrite your understory?
>
> How has your soul or personality been affected by trauma or other life experiences?

Matt's Notes

The overstory and understory concepts are useful tools in helping clients separate their struggles from their personality and who they are as people. Asking clients to reflect on how others perceive them provides them with an opportunity to see how labels they internalize become part of the self-image. The goal is to help them understand that they are not bad or unworthy of a good life. Instead their problems are results of past trauma and with work, their pain and suffering are part of a greater journey to wisdom and strength.

Cousineau's quote and the concept of the soul opens up the opportunity to engage in a deeper spiritual discussion. For many of my clients, a reconnection to religion, faith, or spirituality was a critical step in their healing journey. This chapter provides a great opportunity to talk about spirituality in ways that are best for your client populations.

Chapter 13: Challenges, Addiction, and Trauma

Tragically, for too many of us, bad habits and addiction are part of our journey into darkness. It seems like no matter how much we want to change or try to kick these habits, they haunt us, and their consequences make it hard to live the life we want to live. To begin our exploration of trauma's relationship to habits and addiction, let's start with a quote from author and physician Dr. Gabor Mate (2012)

The question is never 'Why the addiction?' but 'Why the pain?'

As psychology gains a greater understanding of the unconscious, it becomes clear that three instinctual motivators profoundly influence our behaviors. These instincts are to avoid physical or psychological pain, to seek pleasure, and to do both in the most energy-efficient way possible. While these instincts have served humans well historically, they can also lead to many of the unhealthy and self-destructive behaviors that keep us from living the life we want for ourselves and our families (Lisle & Goldhammer, 2003).

Energy Efficiency

If we do not consciously choose to act in new and novel ways, we are likely to unconsciously repeat the behaviors that we relied on in the past. Think about your day today; how much of it is like yesterday and the day before and the day before that? It is human nature to repeat behaviors, as it saves our brain a great deal of energy, versus considering every possible action for every choice that confronts us throughout our day.

If we repeat behaviors over a sustained period, they become habits. Every time we repeat a habit, it reinforces the brain structures that support the associated action. As these structures strengthen, the brain needs less energy to engage in the behaviors associated with the habit (Lisle & Goldhammer, 2003).

A great example of this is brushing our teeth in the morning. Most of us do not need to write a note for ourselves to remember to brush our teeth. Instead, somewhere in our morning routine, we pick up our toothbrush and toothpaste, and our teeth get brushed. Few of us ever have the conscious thought that now would be the perfect time to brush our teeth.

This ability to form habits helps us navigate the world efficiently and saves energy for more demanding or novel tasks. Unfortunately, for those of us with traumatic pasts, this efficiency often leads to harmful habits and reactive ways of interacting with the world. Combined with the motivation to avoid pain and seek pleasure, this drive for efficiency often leads to destructive habits and behaviors that leave us isolated and in continuing cycles of trauma and pain.

Seek Pleasure

Another powerful instinct is to engage in behaviors that bring us pleasure. We feel drawn to things that make us feel good. Once we experience pleasure from an activity, our brain becomes highly motivated to repeat the behavior and re-experience the associated good feeling.

Pleasure and joy are elusive for those who experienced repeated trauma. Relationships and the world become a source of pain instead of comfort. This exposure to pain leads us instinctually to look for happiness from unhealthy sources, such as drugs and other risky behaviors (Siegel, 2011).

Many people can drink or get high without a lot of negative consequences. The same substances that enhance the lives of some destroy the lives of others. What differentiates those who can get positive experiences from drugs versus those who go down the road of addiction? One answer to this question is unresolved trauma (Mate & Levine, 2012).

Avoid Pain

Let's spend a little more time talking about the pain associated with traumatic experiences. Maybe the most influential motivator of all is the avoidance of pain. Pain is electrical impulses in our brain telling us to get away from the thing causing this reaction. Both physical and emotional pain are processed similarly in the brain, and elicit a robust response to do something to eliminate the pain (Mate, 2010).

For someone with an unresolved history of trauma, pain is a constant companion. Trauma often manifests as physical pain in the body and contributes to a range of medical issues, including chronic pain, headaches, and even cancer. Drugs serve as a temporary relief from physical pain.

Trauma also steals our sense of worth and replaces it with the psychological pain of shame. How could one person treat another in such horrible ways? This question haunts those of us who have experienced physical, sexual, and emotional abuse. Not only are we left with the physical pain of violence, but we experience psychological pain that remains long after the physical wounds heal.

The emotional pain of trauma leaves us feeling like the trauma was our fault or even that we caused the trauma to happen. We face some tough questions: "If I'm unlovable, then why wouldn't my partner hit me?" "If I've failed in everything I've given my all to, why would I apply for a part-time job?" "If I've only ever gotten the message that I'm not good enough, why would I expect someone to love me?"

Traumatic pain can destroy a favorable view of one's self as a healthy and good human being. Instead, we feel that we are unworthy of a fulfilled life. Feeling unworthy has consequences well beyond just a painful and pessimistic view of self. To make a positive change in our life, we need to believe we are worthy of the rewards that result from the change.

Trauma and a sense of unworthiness can keep us stuck in destructive behavior patterns long after the trauma is over (Miller & Rollnick, 2013; Siegel, 2011). Feelings of unworthiness and shame directly contradict the sense of self-confidence needed to make a difficult change. Lack of confidence immobilizes us.

It is in this pain that we might reach out for a drink or drug, trying to escape our past or present hardship. The relief the drug offers motivates us to use again, again, and again. Soon this escape becomes its own prison, as addiction takes hold and life becomes organized around getting high.

> What positive habits have you developed?
>
> What habits do you wish you could stop? What do you think has prevented you from ending these habits?
>
> For both positive and negative habits, can you identify how they were created to avoid pain or increase pleasure?
>
> How would changing habits improve your life?

Trauma and Addiction

Few things are as effective as drugs at bringing one pleasure and relieving pain. For someone struggling with the psychological and physical pain associated with trauma, drugs are a quick and relatively cheap escape, at least in the short term. Drugs check off all the boxes: they kill pain and bring pleasure, and they do both very efficiently. Too often though, our short-term escape turns into a problem or addiction.

Traumatized individuals are five times more likely to experience addiction (Mate & Levine, 2012). Addiction leads to behaviors that put us at risk of experiencing additional trauma through the destruction of relationships, loss of home and employment, physical deterioration, and social isolation. A short-term increase in pleasure and escape from pain, unfortunately, has severe long-term consequences.

Three things are required for an addiction. First, we need a susceptible organism. In our situation, the organism is a human being. There is evidence that genetics could make some people more susceptible than others. However, all humans have the potential to become addicted; if ten people start using heroin daily, then after a month, we are likely to have ten people addicted to heroin (Mate & Levine, 2012).

Second, addiction necessitates a drug or a behavior with addictive potential. Not all drugs or behaviors have equal chances for addiction. However, pretty much any behavior or drug that promotes intense feelings of pleasure can lead to addiction.

Finally, addiction requires stress. Trauma is a form of very intense stress. A critical study coming from Vietnam veterans returning to the United States helps shine a light on the role of stress and trauma in addiction. Most everyone would agree that war, in general, is often traumatizing. Additionally, Vietnam was not a proud moment in United States' history. For the first time, the US lost a war, and instead of parades, many soldiers took the brunt of the country's frustration when they reentered their communities (Robins, Helzer, & Davis, 1975).

Coming home from Vietnam, 1 in 5 soldiers met the criteria for addiction, mainly to narcotics. For many, drugs allowed the soldier to escape the horrors of Vietnam, even for just a brief time. In other words, the traumatic stress of war and easy access to drugs resulted in tens of thousands of veterans coming home addicted to hard drugs. As far as the military and public-health infrastructure were concerned, this spelled a disaster. However, something very different happened.

When the stress of war no longer existed, 95% of the soldiers meeting the criteria for addiction showed no signs of addiction to any substance when they returned home. This recovery rate is something that is rarely achieved by substance-abuse programs. Addiction and stress go hand and hand. Rarely does addiction exist without high levels of stress. Trauma is the most intense type of stress and leads people to find relief from the pain and seek some pleasure where they can find it (Robins, Helzer, & Davis, 1975).

Neurobiology of Addiction

Two chemicals are essential to our understanding of addiction. Dopamine is a hormone and neurotransmitter that elicits a sense of pleasure. Experiences, people, and activities that bring us joy result in dopamine release, which motivates us to want to repeat that experience. Most drugs flood the brain with large amounts of dopamine, creating very intense pleasurable experiences.

The second type of chemical is endorphins. Endorphins reduce the experience of pain in the brain. Human-made chemicals that act like endorphins are called opioids. Morphine or Oxycontin are examples of common opioids that operate in much the same way on our bodies as natural endorphins.

Unfortunately, the traumatized brain is fertile ground for drug use to develop into addiction. Unresolved trauma decreases the number of dopamine and endorphin receptors in the brain. Trauma results in a neurobiology that cannot take in the same amount of dopamine and endorphins compared to someone without a traumatic history. The decrease in receptors helps explain the hopelessness and depression many people experience after traumatic events (Mate & Levine, 2012).

Here we'll use a simple example to demonstrate the relationships between addiction and trauma. The example uses a life satisfaction scale where 100 is someone extremely satisfied with their lives, and a 1 is someone clinically and severely depressed and wholly unsatisfied with life. No one knows how many active dopamine and endorphin receptors are in the brain, but for the sake of simplicity in this example, we are going to say that every point on the scale equals 1 trillion open dopamine and endorphin receptors. The brain will open the number of receptors it needs to connect with the normal amount of dopamine and endorphin release in the body on a typical day.

For this example, we will highlight two individuals. Jeff experiences life at an 80 on the life scale, due to great friends, a stable and meaningful job, and a family that loves him. Jeff has 80 trillion active dopamine and endorphin open receptors. Travis experiences life at a 20, due to unresolved past trauma, stress associated with poverty, and unhealthy relationships. He only has 20 trillion open dopamine and endorphin receptors.

Jeff and Travis go to a party. Neither have ever done cocaine, but both try some at the party. The dopamine and endorphin flood boosts Jeff's 80 up to a 90 during the high. This high is a delightful experience for Jeff; he is more social and awake, and he dances all night long. Jeff wakes up the next day, returning to an 80.

Being an 80, Jeff feels good and happy that he had a blast at the party. But this experience is one of many that brings pleasure into Jeff's life. Snowboarding, sex, hanging out with friends, going to concerts, and other experiences have also flooded his system with dopamine and endorphins in the past, eliciting a great overall experience around these activities that he would also rate a 90 or higher. So, while he might use again, the pull back to the drug is not necessarily that great.

Now consider Travis, who lives life at a 20 and is experiencing a high level of emotional pain and stress. He uses cocaine at the same party as Jeff, and cocaine brings Travis' experience of life from a 20 to a 90. Travis has had very few positive life experiences, and the 90 he felt from the cocaine is the best he ever remembers feeling in his entire life.

Waking up the next day back at 20 feels terrible as the pain and stress replace the euphoric fun of the night before. This euphoric experience results in a strong motivation to use again. While Jeff might do cocaine in the future if it is at a party he attends, Travis' natural instincts to seek pleasure and avoid pain will likely get him looking for another high soon to feel that 90 again.

Let's say Travis does find a group of people who use cocaine several times a week. The second time he uses he might get back up to the 90, but from there, the cocaine high only gets him to a 70, and then a 50. Why is his pleasure decreasing?

Travis' brain has established that 20 life satisfaction is normal, and has adjusted his biology to have 20 trillion open dopamine and endorphin receptors to maintain this baseline. If everything else in Travis' life stays at a level 20, such as his job, social interactions, and living conditions, his brain will feel like something is very wrong when he uses cocaine, as it experiences the flooding of these chemicals as an imbalance.

The brain is designed to maintain a balance between itself and the environment. It attempts to reestablish its baseline of 20 by reducing the number of open dopamine and endorphin receptors. Instead of 20 trillion, Travis' receptors decrease to

15 trillion. Cocaine use has now decreased Travis' baseline number of receptors, which leads to consequences in his life, both while sober and while high.

When he is sober, Travis' brain can now take in a fourth less dopamine and endorphins. This reduction will result in a decrease in quality of life, increased irritability, higher levels of depression, a sense of social alienation, extreme fatigue, and other physical and emotional pain. Roughly, you can compare Travis' physical and emotional state when he is not high to a terrible hangover. We call this withdrawal. As with a hangover, one way to feel better is to use drugs again, which eliminates the withdrawal symptoms in the short term.

The other consequence of going from 20 trillion to 15 trillion dopamine and endorphin receptors is that, from this lower baseline, Travis needs more cocaine to get back up to the 90 of his first high. This ability to do more drugs without experiencing the same high as the first time is called tolerance. This is the reason many people overdose. Most people do not overdose because they want to die. Instead, they are aggressively trying to feel as good as they felt the first few times they did the drug.

Here, Travis enters the addiction cycle, which can rapidly control all aspects of his life. Travis feels worse and worse when he is not high, and he needs increasing amounts of cocaine to achieve any feeling of pleasure and to alleviate withdrawal symptoms. This increase in use results in even more significant deactivation of dopamine and endorphin receptors, increasing negative withdrawal symptoms, lowering life satisfaction even further, and requiring more cocaine to feel pleasure and eliminate the pain of withdrawal (Mate & Levine, 2012). And so on, and so on, and so on.

Eventually, Travis might get down to 5 trillion receptors, and he will need an even more substantial amount of cocaine just to get back up to his original 20 baseline. Here is the other part of the addiction cycle. As Travis uses more, it isn't only cocaine that is impacting his ever-decreasing experience of life. He might lose his job, friends and family, housing, social status, physical appearance, and self-worth. So not only is cocaine itself lowering Travis' life satisfaction baseline, but the social consequences of the addiction are also reducing it.

Addiction and Neurobiology

In addition to the impact on dopamine and endorphin levels in the brain, addiction also affects both grey and white matter. White matter is a fatty tissue that increases the efficiency of communication between brain cells and different areas of the brain. White matter naturally increases with age, allowing greater levels of mastery, expertise, and wisdom as we get older. Addiction limits or stops the formation of this age-related white matter. This lack of white matter explains why some people who have used for years might seem stuck in some earlier developmental stage, years behind their chronological age (Mate & Levine, 2012).

If Travis started to use cocaine at 15, parts of his brain might not develop much beyond this age. White matter is also critical to our ability to be flexible with our decision making, our ability to learn new knowledge, skills, and behaviors, and our ability to adapt to new life situations. The lack of white matter just exacerbates many of the symptoms of trauma as brain function becomes further inhibited.

Grey matter makes up much of the physical material in our brains, including brain cells. The effects of addiction on grey matter are just as critical. Brain scans reveal that the number of years of addiction correlates to a decrease in grey matter in the cortex and prefrontal cortex, both key to success in relationships, school, employment, and most other aspects of life. Addiction can damage the brain and, at the same time, prevent neurogenesis, or the creation of new neurons, which is how the brain naturally repairs damage (Mate & Levine, 2012).

When we put the pieces of trauma and addiction together, a devastating reality emerges. Unresolved trauma dramatically increases the likelihood of addiction by decreasing the number of open dopamine and endorphin receptors, thus also decreasing life satisfaction. Addiction damages the very parts of the brain needed for recovery and for making new life decisions and choices that can lead to kicking the addiction.

The social consequences of addiction increase pain and decrease pleasure in life. Getting high provides a short respite, not only from withdrawal, but also from the painful reality of addiction. The person might not have developed the age-related brain maturity critical to insight and the volition needed to change destructive behavior.

Finally, even if Travis gains sobriety, the brain is in danger of relapse. Unless there is an opportunity to change his environment, there will be constant reminders of use. These reminders trigger a dopamine release that the brain associated with the pleasures of the high, making relapse an ever-present struggle in recovery. Reconsider the quote

The question is never 'Why the addiction?' but 'Why the pain?' (Mate, 2012).

The pain of trauma results in suffering, and the person turning to drugs is looking for relief. Unfortunately, their brain is set up to become addicted, leading down a path of darkness to what Campbell calls the abyss. There is always hope, but to journey out of the abyss, the hero needs help and support.

Science demonstrates why getting out of an addiction is so difficult. The good news is that any brain can change and heal over time.

> Can you identify times in your life that pain or stress has led you to use drugs or alcohol as a coping skill?
>
> Have drugs or alcohol ever become your primary way to cope with stress or pain?
>
> Can you list other coping skills that you can utilize instead of drugs or alcohol?

Matt's Notes

This chapter has a lot of material. If you decide to include it in your discussions on the hero's journey, you might consider covering this content in more than one sitting. I found that a deeper understanding of addiction serves as a warning for those without struggles with drugs. For those struggling with addiction, it helps them recognize it as a biological condition instead of a personal defect.

The goal of the first part was to focus on the unconscious motivators; this is designed to help clients identify reactive behaviors and negative consequences of those behaviors. The hope is to provide insight that many causes of their struggles are due to instinctual responses.

For those working with client populations struggling with addiction or at risk of addiction, you may want to spend more time focusing on the science presented in this chapter. As with the unconscious motivator section, we want people to see their behaviors as reactions to their trauma or life situation, and less a reflection on who they are as people. Again, we emphasize separating the person from their problem. They are not addicts; they are people struggling with addiction, which is much more than just their drug use.

Chapter 14: The Hero, the Mentor, and the Abyss

Trauma, suffering, and challenges plague the hero's journey. At some point, these adverse situations and events overwhelm our hero. The light fades, and darkness appears to have complete victory. Campbell (1949) terms this low point the abyss of spiritual and emotional death. The Oxford Dictionary (2017) defines the abyss as

A wide or profound difference between people and the regions of hell, conceived of as a bottomless pit.

In the abyss, the overstory, or what others see, is a life of failure and struggle. The understory, or what is happening to the hero on an emotional and spiritual level, is one of suffering and pain. To the outsider, who is just seeing the overstory, the hero seems to be making one terrible choice after another and has, for some reason, chosen a life that no rational human being would desire.

For some, the abyss is a physical environment that they are attempting to survive every day. War, homelessness or extreme poverty, or living in a violent situation becomes a hell on earth. Daily life for these people carries with it the constant threat of trauma. Survival takes every ounce of their energy and time.

The abyss for others is an internal state. Maybe their life and overstory appear fine to an outsider, but inside they are in extreme pain. Intense states of anxiety and depression resulting from trauma often lead to suicidal thoughts or other acts of self-harm. Even though this abyss is hidden, it is every bit as powerful.

"Losing one's mind" is a scientific tragedy of the abyss. The mind is used here to describe our ability to rise out of survival mode, control our unconscious instincts, and strategically plot our escape from the hopelessness of our situation. The mind relies on many factors; most prominent is the prefrontal cortex, which is unfortunately damaged by trauma and addition. The mind is inaccessible when we are in survival mode.

With limited access to the mind, there is a loss of autonomy, or the ability of the mind to influence behaviors, emotions, or to make new life decisions. Trauma forces us into a survival state, helping us to manage dangerous environments, as it keeps us alert and ready for action. However, due to underactivation of the thinking parts of the brain, trauma can take away the mind's ability to delay gratification, efficiently problem solve, and see the impact of adverse behavior on ourselves and others. At the low point of the journey, we lose all hope that things will get better (Miller & Rollnick, 2013; Siegel, 2011).

One of the characteristics that distinguishes trauma from mere stress is that trauma requires help from others to overcome. The more we learn about trauma, the more we understand that few people can, or should be expected to, emerge from the abyss without tremendous help from caring and compassionate people. Needing other people is no sign of weakness; it just means that we are human beings.

In addition to the research evidence that we need another's help to recover from trauma and get out of the abyss, Campbell found that every great and compelling hero he studied in the mythologies of the word needed someone in their darkest moments (Wright, 2011). "Mentor" is a word Campbell uses to describe a person who helps the hero emerge from the abyss. The origin of the word "mentor" helps to demonstrate their role, as it comes from the Greek root men – to think, remember, counsel – and the Indo-European word mens, for "mind" (Cousineau, 2001).

The mentor is the counselor of the mind. In the hero's journey, all cultures recognize that it is the entry of the mentor into the story that changes the hero's desperate situation.

In our modern society, mentors go by different titles, such as case manager, nurse, therapist, social worker, friend, and teacher. Mentors can also be family members, friends, someone at your church, or a sponsor in a 12-step program. It is often hard for those who experience trauma to accept this help due to their history of being hurt by people they trusted. Despite being let down in the past, finding someone in whom you can place confidence is a crucial aspect of starting to turn your life around and emerging from the abyss.

Accepting help is not always easy. We live in a society that expects us to solve our problems and handle our challenges without burdening other people. The intensity of trauma makes it nearly impossible to recover fully without help from someone who cares about us and our future. The hero is not weak; the hero is overwhelmed by trauma, suffering, and challenges that no human can overcome alone.

Whether we are talking about the heroes of mythology or a person suffering from trauma, the story of their life changes when they accept help from another. Trauma often makes it difficult for us to trust people with stories of our pain and suffering. Few understand the courage it takes to reach out to another for help when we are in the abyss. It is out of this courageous act of letting another into our world that we start the healing part of our story and notice the light of hope shining through the darkness.

> Think about heroes in books or movies; at their darkest moment who came into their lives to help them see hope and change their present situations?
>
> What role did the mentor play in this hero's story? How did the mentor help the hero out of their abyss?
>
> What do you think stops people from reaching out for help when they are struggling?
>
> Can you identify people in your life who can serve as mentors? How can you reach out and ask for help?

Matt's Notes

The goal of this chapter is to help clients understand that needing help is not a sign of weakness or a lack of strength. Having people start by thinking of heroes in fiction, mythology, or religion allows them to think about how these "strong" heroes needed help. Thinking about this first can set the right mindset for exploring how reaching out for help is also a critical part of their journey.

You can integrate the information on social networks presented in Chapter 9. Having clients build a team for the next steps of their journey is a critical outcome of this chapter. The client might not want to tell all the people on their team about their struggles, which is fine. Support is the critical piece to this stage of the journey.

Chapter 15: Establishing Hope

We have come to the point in the journey where the hero finds the strength to emerge from the abyss and begins to rewrite their overstory and understory. In Campbell's model, the abyss is so painful and dark that the hero experiences spiritual and emotional death. There is no light or hope until the hero connects with a mentor. It is at this moment in every myth in which the tide turns, and the hero first sees a spark of hope for a future much better than their present. The mentor assists the hero to transcend emotional and spiritual death and to rise with tremendous strength, to take on the challenges that before seemed impossible to overcome.

Hope is the belief that the future will be better than the present and past. In the abyss, we're forced to focus on survival, which prevents us from thinking too far into the future. The mentor's role is to help us find the resources and strengths within ourselves to start living a new life. This new life requires us to use the resiliency we mustered to survive our trauma and the abyss, turning it into energy for change and transformation.

The power of hope has two critical elements in the hero's journey. First, hope is concrete and tangible. For some it might mean improved housing conditions, food security, getting kids back from social services, going back to school, or kicking a habit or addiction. Hope entails that our future lives look very different from our past experiences of struggle and hardship.

The second element of hope is the realization that we are people of tremendous strength and resiliency. Weak people do not survive the abyss. The hero is a hero because they do not give up when confronted with hardship and suffering. The hero wakes up every morning and faces life. In surviving, we might not always be proud of our actions; however, we were able to survive things that destroy many people.

When the hero meets the mentor, recovery begins primarily as a mission of discovery. Trauma and the abyss rob us of our ability to see ourselves as strong and worthy people. This theft leaves many with a victim mindset. When we are in this mindset, we judge ourselves harshly and can spend a great deal of energy beating ourselves up over past setbacks. We feel like there is something inherently wrong with us; for some reason, other people were born with superior characteristics that we did not receive, which feels like a curse.

The victim mindset keeps us stuck in patterns of negative thoughts, emotions, and behaviors. In this mindset, struggles or setbacks elicit great frustration and anger or depression and resignation. When we struggle to see our strengths, it is difficult to find hope for a better future (Dweck, 2006).

In contrast, people who have what is called a growth mindset are more likely to make positive changes and live the life they aspire to live. Those with this mindset see themselves as results of the effort they put into improving their situation. The harder we work at something, the more likely we are to achieve our goals. When we have a growth mindset, we realize that setbacks are part of every change effort and that goals worth accomplishing require us to overcome challenges along the way (Dweck, 2006).

Those with growth mindsets realize that they can accomplish amazing things with the right mix of effort and resiliency. They start to see themselves as people of value and worth, with something positive to contribute to their families, friends, and the broader community. When we view our life as a result of the effort and energy we put into achieving our goals, we thrive and increase our chances of living the life we want to live.

The first step in establishing a growth mindset is to realize when you are in the victim mindset. When you catch yourself ruminating on past failures or beating yourself up, do your best to say to yourself, "I'm in the victim mindset." This statement sounds like a small thing, but it is a crucial step. When we identify and label a thought pattern or emotional response, we gain control over it and can stop it.

Once you identify that you are in the victim mindset, the next step is to ask yourself, "What actions can I take to improve my situation?" To change our lives, we are challenged to address many things over a period of time. Every meaningful change starts when we identify actions we can take in the present that serve as critical steps on that journey to claiming the life we deserve.

The victim mindset is a natural response to trauma. Anyone who experiences trauma is a victim of something they could not stop or control. There is nothing wrong with having a victim mindset after a traumatic event. However, recovery from trauma requires us to take actions to ensure that the victim mindset does not become a permanent way of viewing ourselves. For those in the abyss, the victim mindset might dominate our thinking. No matter how long we have been in this mindset, our goal is to shift from victim mindset to the growth mindset or from victim to survivor to hero!

Tell me about a time where you felt great strength.

Are there any spiritual, historical, or modern heroes who have particular strengths that inspire you?

If the next five years go well for you, tell me what your life will look like.

Think about a tough change you made in the past; what strengths did you utilize to make this change?

Are there specific situations that put you in the victim mindset where you are hard on yourself? How do you act when you fall into the victim mindset?

What are some areas that you can put effort into that could improve your life?

Matt's Notes

Shedding the victim mindset is a critical part of the journey to post-traumatic growth. Many clients will feel attached to this way of thinking, as being a victim allows them to avoid reflecting on the pain and consequences of their past or present behaviors. We need to help them realize that the important thing is how they move forward into a different future.

I use victim mindset here instead of the fixed mindset I used in the book. I find clients better identify with the concept of the victim in their self-talk and in the actions and words of others. You can easily expand this chapter into a more extensive discussion about fixed and growth mindsets if it fits your client population.

Chapter 16: Alchemy of Transformation

In our journey with the hero, we have reached the critical point of transformation. It is at this point that the resiliency used to survive the trauma and resulting pain and suffering transforms into strength and wisdom, or something we will call post-traumatic growth. This transformation involves social changes to your life situation, physical changes to the structure and functioning of your brain, and for many, changes in your spirituality as well.

Complementary to the hero's journey, there is another ancient practice steeped in mythology that captures the incredible transformation we will examine in this chapter. Alchemy involves transforming something without value into something of great importance. Alchemy is best known as the quest to turn lead into gold, but the history and mythology around alchemy are much more profound. Alchemy involved a personal and spiritual quest into the nature of how human beings interact with the world. Alchemists spent their lives in search of profound knowledge and wisdom, and they had to have strength to be worthy of the life.

Today many view alchemy as a pseudoscience and a foolish endeavor; however, alchemy was the foundation for chemistry, and chemistry the basis for the scientific revolution.

This revolution included physics, biology, and nearly every other natural science. Most scientists can trace their professional roots back to the alchemist's laboratory. One of the most famous alchemists was Isaac Newton, who is also one of the founders of modern physics and still considered one of the smartest men to have ever lived.

For the hero beginning to emerge from the abyss, something incredible is happening on both spiritual and physical levels. On the physical level, the traumatized brain is healing through neuroplasticity, which describes the brain's ability to change and adapt over time. A brain once riddled with mental illness, emotional dysregulation, and addiction transforms into something healthy and powerful.

The alchemy of neuroplasticity is astounding. Through hope, new and healthier behaviors, and support from others, the chemical makeup of the brain changes and our hero returns from the darkness to the light. As the brain heals, the trauma no longer dominates the mind, and pain and suffering give way to a new strength. Overcoming trauma, addiction, homelessness, poverty, and violence are some of the most difficult challenges in the human experience, which is why I do not hesitate to use the word hero to describe those who emerge from these traumatic lives.

For many, the transformation is also spiritual. Some gain strength by reconnecting to the faith of their childhood. Others discover that connecting to a higher power gives them the courage to face the trauma of their past. Those of particular beliefs view their transformation as not only one of body and mind, but also soul and spirit.

Usually through a mix of resources, changes in living situations, connecting with a mentor and other caring people, and personal motivation for a better life, the hero finds the strength and energy to gain control of their emotions and behaviors. The mind starts to emerge, as the hero can recognize and control their unconscious instincts of avoiding pain and seeking pleasure. Transformations begin with a few small steps; the momentum from these successes gives them the confidence to take on harder challenges and more significant life changes.

It is at this critical point where many find it beneficial to connect with another type of mentor in the form of a mental-health professional. Seeing an expert with the right training in trauma treatment helps the hero to face the demons of their past and take power away from the victim mindset, old habits, toxic emotions, and thought patterns. This relationship is critical, as our past trauma can pull us back into the abyss and victim mindset at any time. Life changes and addressing trauma come together to give the hero the tools needed to gain the wisdom and strength necessary to thrive well into the future.

> Think about a hero in the movies, books, or real life; how did they transform their lives to overcome their challenges?
>
> What role did their spiritually play in their transformation?
>
> What support did they get from other people to help them transform their self and their life?

If you could wave a magic wand and transform something in your life, what would you transform? If I took away the wand, what would need to happen to make this transformation a reality?

If you could wave a magic wand and transform something about yourself, what would you transform? If I took away the wand, what would need to happen to make this transformation a reality?

Matt's Notes

This chapter is flexible, depending on what you have already taught clients about trauma and the brain, as featured in earlier chapters. If you have not introduced information on neuroplasticity, brain function, and epigenetics, this would be a good time to include it. If you have presented it, alchemy provides an excellent analogy to get clients thinking about their hero's transformation and their own.

Chapter 17: Transformation: The Alchemy of Mindfulness Part I–Mindful Practice

As we have followed our hero from normal life through trauma, suffering, challenges, the abyss, meeting the mentor, hope, and transformation, it becomes apparent that this journey is one of pain, resiliency, and survival. Just like the mythological heroes, we need help to emerge from the abyss and turn our pain into wisdom, strength, and post-traumatic growth. Transformation is not something one can realize in just a few hours or days. For some, transformation can take years; however, through each step of the process, there are strengths gained and challenges met, and we experience incremental improvements in our quality of life.

Mythologic heroic acts come out of a place of inner strength and calm that the hero creates within themselves. While we often focus on the physical feats of courage, we should not overlook the mental and emotional fortitude of the hero. The power of the mind is as mighty as any sword or magical spell.

Mindfulness is a crucial element in the alchemy of neuroplasticity. We will use mindful practice to strengthen the mind to the point where it gains the power to overcome the thought patterns and addictions of the biological brain.

Practicing mindfulness provides another crucial benefit, in that it repairs the brain areas damaged by trauma (Siegel, 2007).

Mindfulness strengthens the mind through the intentional act of focusing attention toward healthier and more productive behaviors and ways of thinking. Without focused attention, the brain operates on autopilot, unconsciously reacting to things in the environment, choosing the most efficient course of action based on what we have always done in the past: what brings the most pleasure and what reduces pain.

Daniel Siegel (2011) offers one of the best descriptions of the power of mindful awareness:

> With mindful awareness, the flow of energy and information that is our mind enters our conscious attention and we can both appreciate its contents and come to regulate its flow in a new way. Mindful awareness... actually involves more than just simply being aware: It involves being aware of aspects of the mind itself. Instead of being on automatic and mindless, mindfulness helps us awaken, and by reflecting on the mind we are enabled to make choices and thus change becomes possible.

In the next chapter, we will examine specific skills that provide us with the ability to control our unconscious instincts and make more intentional decisions. Here we will introduce the concept of mindful practice. Mindful practice strengthens the logical prefrontal cortex and calms the fear-based and emotional amygdala.

We engage in mindful practices when we focus all our attention on one thing. Some people focus on their breathing; others focus on a task like brushing their teeth, doing the dishes, or walking; still others find it useful to repeat a saying, word, or prayer. The goal is to limit distracting thoughts and emotions and just focus our attention on one thing. At times, distractions will happen. It is okay if your focus wanders; in fact, it is a natural and vital part of mindfulness practice. The real benefit from mindfulness, especially early on, is gained when we lose focus, catch ourselves, and bring our attention back to our activity, prayer, or breathing (Burdick, 2013).

Sometimes people with traumatic pasts struggle with mindful practice. When they quiet their minds, past traumatic memories rise to consciousness. We want to avoid this if possible, and you should stop the practice if it does occur. If you are just beginning a mindful practice, please choose an activity like counting your breaths or repeating a prayer or positive statement, as this will decrease the likelihood that adverse traumatic memories will come into consciousness.

If you find traumatic memories keep coming up, stop your practice and talk to someone about your experience. There are many options that help people take away the power of these memories. We learn a great deal about ourselves during our mindful practice, and this insight lets us know what type of support we need.

Next we will examine an approach that will help guide your practice when memories or feelings do interrupt your focus. Again, these interruptions are natural and beneficial, as they give us an opportunity to bring our attention back to our breathing, prayer, or counting. When we practice mindfulness, we observe, practice nonjudgment, and label thoughts and feelings. We do not react to the emotion or memory, but return our awareness to our mindful practice.

Observing

The first skill is observing thoughts and feelings. When people practice mindfulness, they are attentive to what is happening in their brain and body. Observing thoughts and feelings is a prefrontal cortex activity. This intentional act strengthens the thinking brain and mind, as it reinforces the ability for strategic thinking and emotional regulation.

Nonjudgment

When we practice mindfulness, we want to keep our mind from jumping to judgment, which is associated with the victim mindset. Strange thoughts and memories will pop into your mind when you practice mindfulness, and these thoughts or memories will carry with them certain emotions. All this is natural. The critical task here is to acknowledge the thought or memory without passing judgment on yourself for thinking it or being distracted.

Labeling

When we are unable to label our emotions, they control us, which often leads us to behave in ways we regret later. If we do not jump to judgment, we can practice labeling our emotions. Emotions lose their power when people assign words to them. When odd memories or thoughts come up, we just state to ourselves, "That is odd" or "I haven't thought about that event or person for years." Practicing labeling during mindfulness will start to have real-world benefits for us, as it helps us be nonreactive to things in our environment.

Nonreactivity

Mindfulness gives us power and control over our behaviors. We accomplish this through nonreactivity. Our mindful practice is a perfect time to develop these skills, enabling us to apply them to other aspects of our lives. When a thought or memory comes up, we do not pass judgment on ourselves; we label what we just experienced and then we let it go. The thought or memory occurred, it briefly interrupted our mindful focus, so we acknowledge it and go back to our final step of acting with awareness

Act with Awareness

Observing, nonjudgment, labeling, and being nonreactive allow us to quickly return our focus and awareness to our breathing or prayer. This return of awareness brings us the benefits of mindfulness, as we are intentionally shifting activation back to the prefrontal cortex. Doing this in our practice will allow us to act with awareness in other situations we face.

Matt's Notes

When you reach this step in the hero's journey, you will want to revisit Chapter 9 in the book, on mindfulness. That chapter will give you a set of strategies for introducing mindful practices and ideas of how to practice with clients. When you get to this stage of the hero's journey, you will want to give clients an opportunity to practice and process the experience with you or the group.

This initial practice in a safe place helps to destigmatize mindfulness and help clients experience the calm that practice elicits. A quick internet search will yield many options for mindful activities and guided meditations that you can implement into a variety of settings. Just a reminder, for those with a traumatic past, you want to engage the brain with counting, a saying, or listening to a guided meditation. The goal is to learn how to focus attention, not to clear the mind.

Chapter 18: Transformation: The Alchemy of Mindfulness Part II–Mindful Coping Skills

Mindfulness practice provides us with a place of internal calm and peace. It is this emotional state, established in our practice, that gives us the ability to bring mindful awareness into everyday life, providing us with control over our emotions and behavior. In this chapter, we will examine how we can use the same skills we implemented during mindfulness practice to regulate our emotions, control our actions, and make meaningful change in our lives. You can think of these skills as the powerful tools of the hero for internal transformation and mastery.

Observing

In a real-world application, observing our emotions and thoughts helps us focus on the choices we face in real time. If we are not observing our thoughts and emotions, we will unconsciously repeat past behaviors and habits without any conscious consideration of other possible choices. Observing thoughts and emotions every minute of the day would exhaust us. Instead, practice observing your internal thoughts and emotional reactions when you are engaged in conversations or in situations that are typically stressful. The goal of observing is to catch ourselves when our emotions or habits are determining our behavior and might be hurting our health or our ability to live the life we desire for ourselves.

Nonjudgment

The second skill is being nonjudgmental of the experience. As mentioned in previous chapters, being abused, neglected, or treated poorly by another person can leave us with a victim mindset, feeling that we are unworthy of love and carrying shame about our actions in the past. The second skill of mindfulness challenges us to be kind to ourselves and stop the harsh self-judgment.

Our thoughts and emotions do not define us as a person. Many of us have gotten good at beating ourselves up. Practicing nonjudgment is a skill that needs repetition to master. Allow yourself to listen to what your brain is doing without passing judgment. Thoughts and emotions are the mere reactions in your brain. It is liberating when we realize that our thoughts and emotions are not nearly as important as how we act them out through our behaviors.

To build the skill of nonjudgment, practice on less serious topics and situations. Notice what people are wearing without judging it as good or bad. Have an entire conversation without passing judgment on the other person; instead, focus on just being present in the moment and paying attention to the other person's words. These little steps will build the capacity to take on the more laborious task of applying nonjudgment to your thoughts, feelings, and behaviors.

Labeling

The third skill is labeling. Emotions lose their power when we assign words to them. The act of labeling emotions provides space for conscious consideration and a more rational reaction to what is going on in the environment. Repeated trauma damages the areas of the brain associated with language. We act out when we are unable to express our emotions. Being able to say things such as "I'm pissed off!", "Thinking about that makes me want to cry," and "I hate that person for how they abused me" are powerful first steps in gaining control over our behaviors and breaking free of our habits and addictions.

Observing and being nonjudgmental provides the opportunity to practice labeling. Just as with the first two skills, labeling is a skill to be built over time. Once we get good at labeling, it will increase our ability to successfully engage in and maintain relationships associated with success in academic and employment settings.

Nonreactivity

The capacity to label emotions allows us to work on the fourth skill of nonreactivity. For many of us, reacting quickly helped us survive highly stressful and traumatic situations. Over time, our brain adapts to support this responsiveness at the cost of areas of the brain that support emotional regulation and cognitive ability. Mastery of this skill requires the mind to strengthen to the extent that it can override habits, old behaviors, and unconscious instincts.

Traditionally, many people viewed reactive behaviors as something we could control. Seeing these actions as choices makes it easy to punish and judge people for exhibiting them, but it does not help them gain control over future outbursts. Nonreactivity is an advanced skill. In order not to react, we first must observe and label the emotion in time to not have a reactive behavioral response. Have patience through this learning curve, as mastery in nonreactivity will require changes in brain structure to support it.

Act with Awareness

The final skill and the goal of mindfulness are to act with awareness. Here we find the free will and ability to change behavior and modify our mindset from the victim to the survivor and hero. Acting with awareness is something that is difficult for most people and will take time to implement successfully in stressful situations. We do not always think about our heroes as calm and reflective people, but when we dig deeper into their stories, we find that most heroes have amazing control over their thoughts, emotions, and actions.

Matt's Notes

Seeing mindfulness as not only a practice but also a set of progressive coping skills was one of my most significant insights in writing the book. I had taught each of these skills in different ways over the years, but too often I wanted clients to jump to nonreactivity and to act with awareness before they mastered previous skills. Now I know that most lacked the brain strength to apply these skills without first learning how to observe, not judge, and label their emotions.

There are several ways to practice these skills; doing so in a group or individual session helps the client build self-efficacy to try them in other situations. Here are some ways to help clients develop these skills.

Observing

- Body scans are great ways for the client to get in touch with what is going on in their body and mind. You can have them start at their feet and notice any tightness or pain. Gradually guide their awareness up the body. You can complete this in just a few minutes, which will provide a practical demonstration of observation.

- Another simple task is to stop the conversation or activity and just do a quick check-in. A question such as, "What thoughts (or feelings) are you having right now?" allows the client to check in with themselves briefly and practice observing in the moment. Make sure you communicate that you are going to do this periodically to practice observing.

- Journaling about their day or after a stressful event or interaction helps the client take an introspective moment. Suggest they write about events that were difficult for them and how their body felt at the during these events. While the ultimate goal is to observe the moment, journaling offers an opportunity to practice, reflect, and build this skill with a little distance from the event.

Nonjudgment

- To develop nonjudgment you want to reinforce the concept of shifting from a victim mindset (or fixed mindset) to a growth mindset or to that of the hero. Many clients will benefit from conversations about their specific negative self-talk. The goal of these discussions is not to convince the client that their self-talk is wrong. Instead, help them identify new messages they can send to themselves when they catch themselves engaging in the victim mindset.

- Another excellent practice activity is to have them talk to another person about a mildly controversial topic. This can make a great group activity. Conversations around sports or TV shows are better than serious political or social issues. The idea is to help them find an area of disagreement with someone and practice listening without judging the other person or getting upset. The more they practice with someone else, the more likely they are not to judge themselves.

Labeling

- Like the other skills, many clients will find it easier to label other people's emotions. Using videos or role playing, and asking clients to label what the people in the examples are feeling, helps them understand this skill. This practice will help them apply labeling in their situation and mental states.

- There are numerous emotion sheets on the internet with facial expressions and labels for emotions and feelings. You can start interactions by having the client identify where they are at emotionally using these sheets, repeating this several times throughout the interaction. Again, explain why you are having them do this activity.

- The cup analogy is an excellent tool for labeling. Saying "My cup is full" is a rudimentary method of labeling. Have clients describe what it feels like when their cups are nearly empty, half full, and overflowing. The next step is to help them develop coping skills for when they sense their cup is filling up. Again, practice this throughout a group or session, letting them know ahead of time why you are doing it.

- Journaling about stressful events or interactions will also be very helpful with labeling.

Nonreactivity and Acting with Awareness

Once clients get to these later skills, our role becomes one of positive reinforcement and processing. Since many of the MI skills require some level of awareness, you can begin conversations about more intense and challenging changes.

A quick note about the last four chapters. They are shorter on purpose. Most groups or individual interactions up to this point face common struggles and obstacles to change and healing. The last steps of the journey are unique to the individual. Your customization and creativity will help build the specifics around the structure I provide in these final chapters.

Chapter 19: Transformation: Mindsight

A core lesson the hero learns is that the successful completion of their journey depends on adopting new ways of thinking about problems that overwhelmed them in the past. Transforming is equal parts healing and changing behaviors to establish the life we desire for ourselves and our families. Healing and change are strongly connected processes.

As we heal the wounds of our trauma, our minds become stronger. A stronger mind allows us to identify old harmful habits, behaviors, and addictions that we need to address. As we address these critical challenges, our mind gains even more strength, allowing us to take on even greater change and challenges in the future.

Mentors remain crucial to this part of our journeys. At this point, we might have a case manager, therapist, medical professional, sponsor, and empathetic friends and family, as we develop a supportive network. Each positive person in our network provides us with energy, wisdom, and the support we need to address challenges, heal from our past trauma, and start to live the life we desire.

Few people heal from trauma without a great deal of support. Few people can make a difficult behavioral change without similar support. Reaching out for help is not a sign of weakness. Instead, it is a signal that we are strong enough to take our challenges head on and maximize our chances of success!

Matt's Notes

This place in the hero's journey is an excellent opportunity to integrate the material from Chapter 8 on the stages of change, presented earlier in this supplement. That chapter combines mindsight strategies into the practical model for working through the stages of change. If you would like to have clients think about behavioral change as part of their transformational process, include that chapter and the concepts presented in Chapter 11 in the book, on mindsight, at this point. In the vast majority of cases, behavioral changes are critical aspects of clients' transformation journeys.

Chapter 20: Transformation: Empowering the Mind to Change the Brain

The hero transforms the resiliency they used to survive the darkness into wisdom that guides them throughout the rest of their lives. The alchemy of healing and transformation shows up in a variety of areas. Our physical health improves, our moods are more favorable, and our thoughts move from being dominated by meeting our basic needs in the present to future aspirations. We begin to think of ourselves in different ways as we abandon the victim mindset. At the same time, our environment starts to improve, maybe we move into a better home, we establish healthy friendships and romantic relationships, we might re-enter the job market or otherwise become financially more secure, and we enjoy life more.

As we gain more control and power in our lives, our mind gets stronger. This strength shows up on brain scans, as we see the prefrontal cortex increasing in size and the overactive emotional and fear-based amygdala becoming less active and decreasing in size. Scientists also have discovered that our DNA starts to change how it expresses itself. Transformation is all-encompassing (Shenk, 2010).

Matt's Notes

In these last steps of the journey, we shift focus from present thinking and change to future aspirations. Depending on the length of time you roll out the hero journey material, some clients probably have taken positive steps toward addressing past trauma or considering behavioral changes. Help them reflect on this success by asking questions like these:

> What positive steps have you made in the last couple of weeks to transform your life situation?
>
> What have been the results of these changes or actions?
>
> If you continue down the transformational path, what positive outcomes do you expect?

For groups or clients who have not gotten to the action stage of change, the following questions are helpful for reflection and eliciting motivation to action:

> What are some possible steps you might take to transform your life and heal from trauma?
>
> What support do you need to start considering the first steps on your journey?
>
> What are some outcomes you expect to achieve if you are able to complete your transformational journey?

Chapter 21: Post-traumatic Growth

We have followed our hero on an epic journey out of normal life, into the darkness of trauma and suffering, and into the abyss of spiritual and emotional death. In that abyss, a mentor appears, and a light of hope illuminates the darkness. Through changes in psychological, social, and environmental realities, the hero goes through a process of transformation. We now arrive at the stage of post-traumatic growth, where our hero steps out of the darkness while holding onto the wisdom and strength gained by the journey.

It is essential here to remember the overstory and understory put forth by Phil Cousineau. As a refresher, Cousineau (2001) states:

> I refer to this mystery as the difference between the 'overstory,' which is the visible plot, and the 'understory,' which is the invisible movement of the soul of the main characters. What is mysterious about mythic stories is how they always meander back to the same place: your soul. In this sense myth is a living force, like the telluric powers that stream through the Earth. It is this mythic vision, looking for the 'long story,' the timeless table, that helps us approach the deep mysteries because it insists there is always more than meets the eye.

Post-traumatic growth is the emergence of a transformed soul or mind with the resiliency and wisdom gained from overcoming trauma and suffering. There is a burst of energy and motivation that comes from understanding that if we can live through the hell of the abyss, we can search for new challenges and start to build the life we aspire to live.

The main character transforms from being unworthy and unable to control their actions to someone with a positive sense of self who has power in their lives. Relationships shift from being dangerous and painful to balanced, with an understanding that some people are wonderful and caring, while others can still cause harm and hurt. Their world also transforms from a dangerous and painful place filled with suffering to one of opportunity. The main character brings to their relationships and the world a tremendous amount of "street smarts" that, mixed with resiliency and strength, allow them to change their overstory as well.

Matt's Notes

Post-traumatic growth is about wisdom and strength. As we approach the end of the hero's journey, we want clients to recognize the power that lies within them. If you are doing these activities in groups, this is a great time to have group members share the strengths they recognize in other group members.

For those struggling to find the motivation to start addressing behaviors or engaging in mental-health services, have them discuss changes they have seen in other people who experienced struggles like those they are going through in their own lives. Another approach is to have them identify heroes in film or fiction and talk about the strength and wisdom those heroes developed through their journey.

Chapter 22: The Return

Our hero's journey is coming to a final transition. At this point, we have witnessed our hero thrust into darkness through trauma. For too many, this ends in the abyss of spiritual and emotional death. Then a mentor comes into the darkness of the abyss and shines the light of hope into the hero's reality. This hope, along with the support and compassion of the mentor, helps the hero transform pain and suffering into wisdom and courage, leading to post-traumatic growth.

The final stage of the journey is a return to normal life. Here, the hero brings the strength and experience gained during the journey into a more stable and fulfilling life. On the surface, in the overstory, this might take the form of full-time employment, permanent housing, release from prison, or regaining custody of children. There are noticeable changes that are visible to everyone who has witnessed the hero's journey.

The changes in the soul, or the understory, might not be as visible, but are just as powerful as the overstory, if not more so. For many people who have taken this journey, there is something in them that calls them to give back and use their strength and courage to help others still suffering in the abyss. For each, this call is different, but most benefit in some way in giving back.

Matt's Notes

Depending on where clients are in their journey, some might struggle to connect with the return. If this is the case, combine this chapter with the previous one, as they both speak to what is possible and will often elicit change talk. It is essential to get here, because we want clients to understand what is possible with hard work. Again, having clients think about a fictional hero's journey provides many with a safe way to explore the return without dwelling on the bleakness of their current condition.

For those further in their journey, the return can entail goal setting and concrete planning. It is a powerful moment when someone shares aspirations and dreams with you or a group. For those at this point, it is crucial to ensure they have support moving forward to help them turn their goals into reality.

Regardless of where groups and individuals are in their journeys, it is essential to celebrate the transformational nature of the human experience. Throughout the process, you should have gotten many small and dramatic examples of change and healing. Make sure you take a moment to recognize the power of these stories and the hope that they provide for all of us.

Conclusions

I hope this supplement helps you find ways to empower clients through knowledge and psychosocial support around essential drivers for healing and change. The concepts presented here realize their full effectiveness when delivered and supported by the spirit of MI and its trauma-informed communication approaches. Trauma and change are powerful concepts that challenge clients to go deep into their experiences and shortcomings. Your support, empathy, and compassion are often the determining factor in whether change and healing happen.

As a reminder, the approaches presented in the supplement, as well as the strategies presented in the book, are tools in your trauma-informed tool belt. These tools are only effective when delivered within the context of a compassionate and strong relationship. As this chart on what drives client outcomes reminds us, the client's success relies on our ability to build a strong partnership, to help them see hope for a better future, and to effectively implement the best practices presented here and in the book.

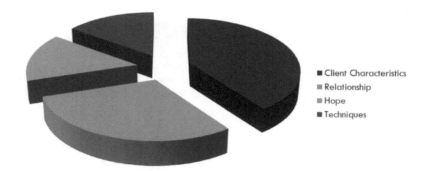

About the Author

Matthew S. Bennett has successfully combined his academic pursuits as a researcher, blogger, and published author with his practical experience developing research-based solutions to improve the health of individuals, organizations, and systems. He has a master's degree in community psychology and executive development (nonprofit management), as well as a master's in business administration in health care. As a sought-after trainer and speaker, Matt's presentations are a dynamic dance of innovative research, practical application, and a passion for the art and science of helping others.

You can find more about Matt's work, his Matt's Mumblings Blog, and the Trauma-Informed Lens Podcast at www.connectingparadigms.org.

Bibliography

Achor, S. (2010). The happiness advantage. New York: Crown Business.

Bale, T. (2015). Epigenetic and transgenerational reprogramming of brain development. Nature Reviews Neuroscience, 16, 332–344; doi:10.1038/nrn3818.

Bennett, M. S. (2017). Connecting paradigms: A trauma-informed & neurobiological framework for motivational interviewing implementation. Denver: A BIG Publication.

Bloom, S. L. (2000). Creating sanctuary: Healing from systematic abuses of power. Therapeutic Communities: The International Journal for Therapeutic and Supportive Organizations 21(2), 67–91.

Bloom, S. L. (2006). Organizational stress as a barrier to trauma-sensitive change and system transformation. A white paper for National Technical Assistance Center for State Mental Health Planning (NTAC).

Bloom, S. L., & Farragher, B. (2011). Destroying sanctuary: The crisis in human service delivery systems. New York: Oxford University Press.

Bloom, S, L., & Farragher, B. (2013). Restoring sanctuary: A new operating system for trauma-informed systems of care. New York: Oxford University Press.

Burdick, D. (2013). Mindfulness skills workbook for clinicians & clients: 111 Tools, techniques, activities, & worksheets. Eau Claire, WI: PESI Publishing and Media.

Campbell, J. (1949). The hero with a thousand faces. Princeton: Princeton University Press.

Centers for Disease Control and Prevention (2016, April 1). Adverse Childhood Experiences (ACEs). Retrieved from http://www.cdc.gov/violenceprevention/acestudy/

Christakis, N. A., & Fowler, J. H. (2009). Connected: The surprising power of our social networks and how they shape our lives. New York: Little, Brown and Company.

Courtois, C. A., & Ford, J. D. (Eds.). (2009). Treating complex traumatic stress disorder: An evidence-based guide. New York: Guilford Press.

Cousineau, P. (2001). Once and future myths: The power of ancient stories in our lives. Boston: Conari Press.

Cozolino, L. (2006). The neuroscience of human relationship: Attachment and the developing social brain. New York: W.W. Norton & Company, Inc.

Cozolino, L. (2010). The neuroscience of psychotherapy: Healing the social brain. New York: W.W. Norton & Company, Inc.

Dweck, D. S. (2006). Mindset: The new psychology of success. New York: Ballantine Books.

Finch, C. E., & Loehlin, J. C. (1998). Environmental influences that may precede fertilization: A first examination of the prezygotic hypothesis from maternal age influences on twins. Behavioral Genetics, 28(2), 101.

Goleman, D. (2006). Social intelligence: The new science of human relationships. New York: Bantam Books.

Haidt, J. (2006). The happiness hypothesis: Finding modern truth in ancient wisdom. New York: Basic Books.

Heath, C., & Heath, D. (2010). Switch: How to change things when change is hard. New York: Broadway Books.

Herman, J. L. (1997). Trauma and recovery. New York: Basic Books.

Hodge, T. (2014). Trans-generational trauma: Passing it on. Charleston, SC: CreateSpace Independent Publishing Platform.

Lakein, A. (1973). How to get control of your time and your life. New York: New American Library.

Langer, E. J. (2009). Counterclockwise: Mindful health and the power of possibility. New York: Random House.

Lewis, G. (2006). Organizational crisis management: The human factor. Boca Raton, FL: Auerbach Publications.

Lipton, B. H. (2006). The wisdom of your cells: How your beliefs control your biology. Louisville, CO: Sounds True, Inc.

Lisle, D. J., & Goldhammer, J (2003). The pleasure trap: Mastering the hidden force that undermines health and happiness. Summertown, TN: Healthy Living Publications.

Marlatt, G. A., Larimer, M. E., & Witkiewitz, K. (Eds.). (2012). Harm reduction: Pragmatic strategies for managing high-risk behaviors. New York: Guilford Press.Mate, G., & Levine, P. A. (2010). In the realm of hungry ghost: Close encounters with addiction. Lyons, CO: The Ergos Institute.

Medina, J. (2014). Your best brain: The science of brain improvement. Chantilly, Virginia: The Great Courses.

Miller, W. R., & Rollnick, S. (2012). Motivational interviewing: Helping people change (3rd ed.). New York: Guilford Press.

Murphy, J. J. (2008). Solution-focused counseling in schools (2nd ed.). Alexandria, VA: American Counseling Association. Retrieved from http://counselingoutfitters.com/vistas/vistas08/Murphy.htm

Nakazawa, D. J. (2016). Childhood disrupted: How your biography becomes your biology, and how you can heal. New York: Atria Books

Ogden, P., Minton, K., & Pain, C. (2006). Trauma and the body. New York: W. W. Norton and Company, Inc.

Oxford English Dictionary. (2017). http://www.oed.com

Parnell, L. (2008). Tapping in: A step-by-step guide to activating your healing resources through bilateral stimulation. Boulder, CO: Sounds True, Inc.

Pierce, J. H. (2006). The owner's manual for the brain: Everyday applications from mind-brain research (3rd ed.). Austin, TX: Bard Press.

Prochaska, J. O., DiClemente, C. C., & Norcross, J. C. (1992). In search of how people change: Applications to addictive behaviors. American Psychology 47,1102.

Robins, L, Helzer, J. E., & Davis, D. H. (1975). Narcotic use in Southeast Asia and afterward, Archives of General Psychiatry 23 (1975): 955-961.

Rock, D. (2009). Your brain at work: Strategies for overcoming distraction, regaining focus, and working smarter all day long. New York: HarperCollins.

Roe, G. (2005). Harm reduction as paradigm: Is better than bad good enough? Critical Public Health, 15(3), 243–250.

Rohn, J. (2010). The treasure of quotes. Dallas, TX: SUCCESS Books.

Rudacille, D. (2011, April 18). Maternal stress alters behavior of generations. Spectrum News. Retrieved from http://spectrumnews.org/news/maternal-stress-alters-behavior-of-generations/

Sapolsky, R. M. (2017). Behave: The biology of humans at our best and worst. New York: Penguin Press.

Schwartz, J. D., & Begley, S. (2002). The mind and the brain: Neuroplasticity and the power of mental force. New York: HarperCollins.

Shenk, D. (2010). The genius in all of us. New York: Doubleday.

Siebert, A. (2005). The resiliency advantage. San Francisco: Berrett-Koehler Publishers Inc.

Siegel, D. J. (2007). The mindful brain. New York: W. W. Norton & Company, Inc.

Siegel, D. J. (2011). Mindsight: The new science of personal transformation. New York: Bantam Books.

Siegel, D. J. (2016). Mind: A journey to the heart of being human. New York: W. W. Norton & Company, Inc.

Stanley, B., & Brown, G. K. (2012). Safety planning intervention: A brief intervention to mitigate suicide risk. Cognitive and Behavioral Practice, 19(2), 256–264.

Wagner, R., & Harter, J. K. (2006). 12: The elements of great managing. New York: Gallup Press.

Wolynn, M. (2016). It didn't start with you: How inherited family trauma shapes who we are and how to end the cycle. New York: Viking.

Wright, H. N. (2011). The complete guide to crisis and trauma counseling: What to do and say when it matters most! Ventura, CA: Regal.

Yehuda, R., Bierer, L. M., Schmeidler, J., Aferiat, D. H., Breslau, I., & Dolan S. (2000), Low cortisol and risk for PTSD in adult offspring of holocaust survivors. American Journal of Psychiatry, 157(8) (August 2000), 1252–1259.

Yehuda, R., Engel, S. M., Brand, S. R., Seckl, J., Marcus, S. M., & Berkowitz, G. S. (2005). Transgenerational effects of posttraumatic stress disorder in babies of mothers exposed to the World Trade Center attacks during pregnancy. Journal of Clinical Endocrinology & Metabolism, 90(7) (July 2005), 4115–4118.

Yehuda, R., Daskalakis, N. P., Bierer, L. M., Bader, H. N., Klengel, T., Holsboer, F., & Binder, E.B. (2015). Holocaust exposure induced intergenerational effects on KDBP5 methylation. Biological Psychiatry, 80(5), 372–380.

Printed in Poland
by Amazon Fulfillment
Poland Sp. z o.o., Wrocław